T0368116

Notes for the Serious Bible Student

Going
Deeper...

Dr. J.R. Chisley

WESTBOW
PRESS®
A DIVISION OF THOMAS NELSON
& ZONDERVAN

WestBow Press books may be ordered through booksellers or by contacting:

WestBow Press
A Division of Thomas Nelson & Zondervan
1663 Liberty Drive
Bloomington, IN 47403
www.westbowpress.com
1 (866) 928-1240

Scripture taken from the King James Version of the Bible.

ISBN: 978-1-9736-1194-3 (sc)
ISBN: 978-1-9736-1195-0 (e)

Library of Congress Control Number: 2017919546

Print information available on the last page.

WestBow Press rev. date: 12/28/2018

Contents

2nd Edition

How to use this book

GETTING TO GRIPS WITH BIBLICAL LANGUAGES

Introduction:

The Bible as we know it today was composed in two main languages: the Old Testament primarily in Hebrew, and the New Testament in a variant of the Greek language known as Koine Greek (which simply means 'common' Greek, since it was the everyday version of the language spoken around the Mediterranean at that time).

These two languages, Hebrew and Greek, are often baffling for modern English speakers, because they are so different to English. They both have different alphabets (the word 'alphabet' is a contraction of the first two Greek letters 'alpha' and 'beta', which themselves evolved from the Hebrew letters 'aleph' and 'beth'), and if that wasn't enough, Hebrew is read from right-to-left, rather than left-to-right (which means that the Hebrew Bible is read from back to front).

Despite the difficulties, becoming familiar with Hebrew and Greek is one way of discovering the amazing depth and poetry of the Scriptures, and thereby to have a better knowledge of God. That is part of the aim of this book. Along with the study of numerous passages of Scripture, this book will also outline the important vocabulary for each lesson, whether in Greek or Hebrew, so helping you to understand the Scriptures in their original languages.

You may be reading this book with a deep knowledge already of the biblical languages, in which case we hope that the lessons and the vocabulary will strengthen that knowledge and bring you ever more, closer to God. However, you may have only just begun to study Greek or Hebrew. So that you can begin using the vocabulary in the lessons straight away, we have prepared a guide to the languages below.

These guides are not intended as replacements for good Hebrew and Greek lexicons and books of grammar, but they will point you in the right direction.

The Hebrew language:

Hebrew	Name	No.
א	Aleph	1
ב	Beth	2
ג	Gimel	3
ד	Daleth	4
ה	He	5
ו	Waw	6
ז	Zayin	7
ח	Heth	8
ט	Teth	9
י	Yod	10
כ	Kaph	20
ל	Lamed	30
מ	Mem	40
נ	Nun	50
ס	Samech	60
ע	Ayin	70
פ	Pe	80
צ	Sadhe	90
ק	Qoph	100
ר	Resh	200
ש	Shin	300
ת	Tav	400

The Hebrew alphabet contains 22 consonants, ranging from *aleph* to *tav* (there are several slightly different forms of consonants that go at the end of words, but for simplicity we will ignore these).

The Hebrew language is written from right-to-left. Because there are no separate characters in Hebrew for numbers, each letter is assigned a number, so *aleph* can also mean 1; *mem,* 40; *shin* 300, and so on.

The most different aspect of Hebrew compared to English is how the vowels are displayed. There are no letters in the alphabet to represent vowel sounds. Instead, there are a series of dots and dashes that are written above and below the consonants to indicate which vowels go with them.

This book will not teach you how to write these vowel sounds, but there are plenty of other resources that will do so. Instead, each Hebrew word in the vocabulary will be written first in Hebrew, and then given an English equivalent, so that you have an idea of how the word is pronounced.

Pronunciation guide:

There are three different groups of vowel sounds: the long vowel, the short vowel, and the reduced vowel. They all have slightly different pronunciations, as shown in the table below:

For each Hebrew word, an equivalent English pronunciation is given. Each word is split into syllables, with dashes between syllables. The stressed syllable in each word is written in CAPITAL LETTERS. For example:

The word 'treaty' would be written TRĪ-tī

The word 'capital' would be written: KAP-i-təl

The word 'oboe' would be written: Ō-bō

The word 'ark' would be written: ĀRK

The word 'foolish' would be written: FŪ-lish

The vowels in these words can be pronounced using the table below:

Long Vowel	Short Vowel	Reduced Vowel
Ā, ā (like 'a' in 'father')	A, a (like 'a' in 'cat')	ă (very short a)
Ē, ē (like 'ay' in 'May'	E, e (like 'e' in 'bet')	ĕ (very short e)
Ī, ī (like 'ee' in 'seem')	I, i (like 'i' in 'bit'	
Ō, ō (like 'o' sound in 'bone')	O, o (like 'o' in 'hot')	ŏ (very short o)
Ū, ū (like 'oo' sound in 'shoe')	U, u (like 'u' in 'put')	
ə - sounded like the first 'a' in 'banana' (a very short, indiscriminate vowel sound)		

The Greek language:

Greek	Name	Sound	No.
A, α	Alpha	A	1
B, β	Beta	B	2
Γ, γ	Gamma	G	3
Δ, δ	Delta	D	4
E, ε	Epsilon	e (like 'pet')	5
Z, ζ	Zeta	Z	7
H, η	Eta	ē (like 'see')	8
Θ, θ	Theta	Th	9
I, ι	Iota	I	10
K, κ	Kappa	K	20
Λ, λ	Lambda	L	30

Μ, μ	Mu	M	40
Ν, ν	Nu	N	50
Ξ, ξ	Xi	X	60
Ο, ο	Omicron	o (like 'dot')	70
Π, π	Pi	P	80
Ρ, ρ	Rho	R	100
Σ,σ,ς	Sigma	S	200
Τ, τ	Tau	T	300
Υ, υ	Upsilon	U	400
φ, φ	Phi	F	500
Χ, χ	Chi	ch (like 'loch')	600
Ψ, ψ	Psi	Ps	700
Ω, ω	Omega	ō (like 'torn')	800

The Greek alphabet contains 24 letters of which 7 are vowels. Many of the letters have an obvious English equivalent, like a, b and p. However, some are represented in English by the sound of a couple of consonants, such as th or ps. There are also two vowels which have no separate English equivalent: eta, or long e, represented by ē; and omega, long o, represented by ō. There is one letter which varies when put at the end of the word: sigma, which changes from σ to ς.

The Greek language is written from left-to-right. Because there are no separate characters in Greek for numbers, each letter is assigned a number, so alpha can also mean 1; *mu*, 40; tau 300, and so on.

An important thing to be aware of is that Greek has no equivalent letter for 'h' in English. The 'h' sound in Greek is only present when the word starts with a vowel, and an accent (called an aspirate, or breathing symbol) is used above it to represent this. The aspirate has two forms: ἀ, a smooth breathing, which shows that no 'h' sound is required (pronounced 'a'); and ἁ, a rough breathing, which requires an 'h' sound, and is pronounced 'ha'.

For example, the Greek word ἄρτος, bread, has a smooth breathing at the start, and is pronounced 'artos' (note the variant of the letter sigma at the end of the word, and don't worry about the other accent over the alpha for now). The Greek word εὑρίσκω, I find, has a rough breathing at the start, and so is pronounced 'heuriskō' (remember, the 'o' at the end is long).

These breathings are used for any word that begins with either a vowel, or the letter rho (which is why the English spelling of the plant 'rhodedendron', which comes from the Greek, has the letter h after the r: it's a rough breathing).

For each Bible lesson from the New Testament, each word will be given in English, then in the Greek form in which it is found in the text, then transliterated into English as in the examples above, and finally given some alternative definitions. Occasionally, the transliterated word may be followed by another word in brackets. This is to indicate the root form of the word, so it can be easily found in a lexicon if required. The roots of many Greek words are obvious with a bit of practice, but some words change markedly depending on the tense and person. In these cases the root form is given as an aide to the student.

Finally, there is no clear consensus on how Koine Greek is pronounced. Keep it simple, say the consonants clearly, and you will be fine. While Greek does have a system of accents, and these have been included for accuracy; they have little bearing on how words are pronounced and can be safely ignored.

Hearing Requires Listening

EXODUS 3:1-12

Introduction:

The word listening is the Hebrew word קָשַׁב, qā-SHAV, which means 'attend, to give attention to.' God attends our cry, and He desires that we attend His call.

The book of Genesis reveals the Divine purpose; the book of Exodus reveals Divine performance. In Genesis we see human effort and failure; in Exodus we see Divine power and triumph.

word of promise	work of fulfillment
a people chosen	a people called
God's electing mercy	God's electing manner
revelation of nationality	realization of nationality

God had related to Abraham that the captivity would take place (Gen. 15:13).

Jacob and His family came down to Egypt around 1875 B.C. They remained 430 years (Ex. 12:40). This would place the time of their departure around 1445 BC (1 Ki. 6:1, Gal. 3:17).

Moses' life was divided into 3 groups of 40 years: 40 years in Pharaoh's palace, 40 years in the desert and 40 years as deliverer.

Translation, transliteration, interpretation:

v.	English	Hebrew	Pronunciation	Alternative meanings
1	backside	אַחַר	a-KHAR	far side

Mt Horeb and Mt. Sinai are different parts of the same mountain.

v.	English	Hebrew	Pronunciation	Alternative meanings
2	in flame	לַבָּה	lab-BĀH	
	fire	אֵשׁ	ĒSH	
	midst	מִתּוֹךְ	mit-TŌKH	from within, from the heart of
	consumed,	אָכַל	ā-KHAL	destroyed

3	turn aside,	רָאָה rā-ĀH	to consider, to behold, to view, aspect
	great sight	מַרְאֶה mar-EH	
	the sight	גָּדֹל gā-DŌL	the strange
	I will now turn	סוּר SŪR	I will go over
5	draw	קָרַב qā-RAV	approach, come near
	standeth	עָמַד ā-MAD	
	Holy ground	קֹדֶשׁ אַדְמַת־ ad-mat - QŌ-desh	
6	hid	סָתַר sā-TAR	and he hid
	look upon	נָבַט nā-VAT	
	He was afraid	יָרֵא yā-RĒ	
7	I have surely seen	רָאֹה rā-ŌH	
	my people	עַמִּי am-MĪ	
	misery	עֳנִי ŏ-NĪ	
	heard	שָׁמַע shā-MA	
	taskmasters	מִצְרָיִם mits-RAYIM	Egyptian slavemasters
8	I am come down	יָרַד yā-RAD	so I came down
	flowing	־תזֻב zā-VAT	
	milk	חָלָב khā-LĀV	(referring to cows and goats, that give milk)
	honey	דְּבַשׁ də-VASH	
9	is come	בּוֹא BŌ	to come in
12	certainly	כִּי KĪ	
	token	אוֹת ŌT	evidence, proof, signal, indication

Lessons from the lesson:

- God introduces Himself as "Elohīm" (the God of power, 6, 12).
- Curiosity may have killed the cat, but Moses' curiosity saved him and his people (3).
- God's appearance in nature, theologically, is called a theophany (4).
- God is still-calling men and women to serve Him (4).
- UnHoly dirt and dust can separate men from the Holy God (5).
- Our God is not a God, but the God; (making use of the definite article) (6).
- God sees, hears, and cares for His people (7).
- God delivers from and to (Egypt to Canaan, 8).
- Sincere prayer ascends to God's throne, and has a sweet aroma (9).

- God is preparing us (often unawares, 10).
- God attends our cry and desires that we attend His call (7, 10).
- God's presence is not limited to a bush (2).
- God's tokens and signs prove and verify His truth (12).

Accepting Responsibility

EXODUS 4:10-16, 27-31

Introduction:

After being called of God, the called must accept the responsibility that goes with it.

It took a lot of convincing before Moses accepted his responsibility. He offered several excuses, the main one being that he was afraid to appear again before Pharoah. God answered each of Moses' excuses, until he had no more. Moses was reluctant; God was determined.

Translation, transliteration, interpretation:

v.	English	Hebrew	Pronunciation	Alternative meanings
10	eloquent	דָּבָר	dā-VĀR	fluent in words, in Egyptian language, to present a case before a King.

Acts 7:22: "And Moses was learned in all the wisdom of the Egyptians, and was mighty in words and in deeds."

After 40 years, Moses could have forgotten some of the language he had learned. The Egyptian language truly was different from Hebrew (Gen. 42:23).

v.	English	Hebrew	Pronunciation	Alternative meanings
	slow of	כָּבֵד	kā-VĒD	
	speech	פֶּה	PEH	
	tongue	לָשׁוֹן	lā-SHŌN	
11	hath made	שָׂם	SĀM	
	mouth	פֶּה	PEH	
	dumb	אִלֵּם	il-LĒM	
	deaf	חֵרֵשׁ	khē-RĒSH	
	seeing	פִּקֵּחַ	piq-QĒAKH	sight
	blind	עִוֵּר	iv-VĒR	
12	thou mouth	פִּיךָ	PĪ-khā	
	and teach thee	הֹרֵי	yā-RĀH	and I will teach you
13	by another	בְּיַד־	bə-YAD	
	you send	שָׁלַח	shā-LAKH	
14	anger	אַף	AF	
	kindled	חָרָה	khā-RĀH	burned

9

God had already spoken with Aaron. These brothers may not have seen each other for 40 yrs.

16	spokesman	לְפֶה	lə-FEH	as mouth
	instead of God	לֵאלֹהִים	lē-lō-HĪM	
27	kissed	נָשַׁק	nā-SHAQ	
28	the signs	אֹת	ŌT	
29	elders	זָקֵן	zā-QĒN	
31	visited	פָּקַד	pā-QAD	inspect, look after
	looked upon	נָבַט	nā-VAT	look attentively
	affliction	עֲנִי	ŏ-NĪ	misery
	worshipped	שָׁחָה	shā-KHĀH	bow self down
	believed	אָמַן	ā-MĒN	remain steadfast

Lessons from the lesson:

- Moses' tongue was slow; sometimes our tongues are too fast, needing to slow down (10). God is able, and He enables (10).
- We don't have to be eloquent to speak and lead for God (10).
- God, who made us, knows more about us than we know about ourselves (11).
- He is the potter, we are the clay.
- God did not make man's mouth as it has become today (11).
- If God is with us, we need not fear (12).
- Man is full of excuses for disobeying God.
- Man's excuses are provocative to God (14).
- Being educated, Moses still needed to be educated (15).
- Moses and Aaron made a good team for God (16).
- God, who called Moses, also called Aaron (even a helper must be called of God).
- Moses and Aaron were equipped with both words and signs, (28).
- God is aware of our afflictions and is worthy of our worship (31).
- God has a purpose for making the deaf, dumb, and blind (11).
- God will not be out done; He is determined (12), Ecc. 4:9-10.

Recognizing True Authority

EXODUS 5:1-9, 22-6:1

Introduction:

The true authority of the children of Israel then and now is God. Pharoah was in control but he was only there temporarily: ultimately, God was still in control; as a matter of fact, God is never out of control. He is the true authority; the world is under His dominion.

Translation, transliteration, Interpretation:

v.	English	Hebrew	Pronunciation	Alternative meanings
1	Afterward (after Aaron had completed the miracles before the elders, 4:30).			

"Thus saith the Lord": this was the manner of introduction of all of the prophets; they were spokesmen for the Lord.

| | feast | חָגַג | khā-GAG | |

Even then, the Jews corporatively, needed to acknowledge their sins to God. Moses didn't give God's Tetragrammaton to Pharoah, but only said that He was the God of Israel.

"My people": here God was acknowledging ownership of the children of Israel.

2	obey	שָׁמַע	shā-MA	
	I know not the Lord	יָדַע	yā-DA	(see 1 Thess. 1:8)
3	hath met with us	קָרָא	qā-RĀ	to meet, to view (God is real, alive)
	we pray	אָנָה	ĀN-nāh	we pray thee, we humbly ask thee, we beg thee

Lest He fall upon us with pestilence or with the sword. This was putting it lightly, without appearing as a threat to the King. It did include Him.

| | fall upon us | פָּגַע | pā-GA | (they both would share in God's displeasure) |

Historians place King Thutmose 3rd reigning 1504-1450, and Amenhotep 2nd reigning around 1445

| 4 | Moses and Aaron were recognized as wise men by the King and were excluded from slavery. | | | |
| | burdens | סָבַל | sā-VAL | to bear |

You are disturbing the people, taking their minds from their work, giving them rest from my work. God had-already told Moses that the King would not let them go: 3:19, 4:2.

7	straw	תֶּבֶן	TE-ven	stubble (straw mixed in with the mortar gave strength to the brick)
8	tale	הֶגֶה	He-geh	utterance
	idle	רָפָה	rā-FĀH	slack, remiss, relaxed
9	vain	שֶׁקֶר	SHE-qer	falsehood, lie

The taskmasters were beaten for failing to meet the King's quota.

22	evil entreated	רַע	RA	

The Hebrew's word for evil has many meanings; vanity, iniquity badness, favouredness (Deut. 17:1), bad report, etc.

Our strength is made perfect in weakness, 2 Cor. 12:9.

Before God's wrath comes His mercy (as in the days of Noah and Enoch).

The same sun that melts the ice hardens the clay; the difference is not the sun's fault.

God had already told Moses that he would be successful (3:12, 20, 21, 22).

23	delivered	נָצַל	nā-TSAL	to snatch, take away
6:1	strong hand	חָזַק	khā-ZAQ	firm, hold fast, hard hand, girding

Lessons from the lesson:

- Instead of taking our burdens to the Lord, we often take them to another, as the Jews did (3).
- Satan never gives up his prey without a struggle (2, Lk. 9:42).
- Don't back down at the first sign of opposition (2).
- God is not to blame for sinner's hard heart; the same sun melts the ice and hardens the clay (2).
- God allowed the King to harden his own heart (8:15).
- Evil often gets worse before it gets better (6-9).
- God used the King's hardheartedness to reveal His power and love (Ex. 9:16; Rom. 9:17).
- God should not be questioned or blamed (22, Rom. 9:20).
- God is never too slow; and definately never too fast (6:1).

Commissioning for Service

LEV. 8:1-13

Introduction:

The book of Leviticus has been called God's manual for His people on how to approach Him and live pleasingly in His sight. The basic principle of law undergirds the whole book. The Greeks called it "Levitikon," 'pertaining to the Levites.' This name was translated to Leviticus in the "Vulgate". The book of Hebrews is a good commentary on the book of Leviticus (see Heb. 7:11).

In this book, "God gave the laws to His people thru Moses" is mentioned some 56 times; and the word "Holy" is there some 90 times. The key command is "ye shall be Holy."

God's law is intended to show man his corruption; and bring conviction for sin. A low view of law brings legalism; a high view of law brings the seeking of grace.

W. Graham Scroggie says "Exodus begins with sinners, Leviticus begins with saints."

Exodus records how Israel became a redeemed nation; Leviticus concerns the cleansing, worship, and service of a redeemed Nation.

At Sinai the Jews were given 5 offerings to make to God (Lev. 7:38, 27:34).

The burnt offering, 1:3-17, 6:8-13.

The meal offering, 2:1-16, 6:8-13.

The peace offering, 3:1-17, 7:11-34.

The sin offering, 4:1-5:13, 6:24-30.

The trespass offering, 5:14-6:7, 7:1-10.

The book of Leviticus is the most legalistic of the OT. It is a handbook for the priests.

Translation, transliteration, interpretation:

v.	English	Hebrew	Pronunciation	Alternate meanings
2	The sons of Aaron were Nadab, Abihu, Eleazar, Ithamar (Lev. 10:1, 16; Num. 3:4).			
	take	לְהַקְרִיב	lə-haq-RĪV	bring, encourage to the duty of priests
	the garments	הַבְּגָדִים	hab-bə-gā-DĪM	

	anointing oil	שֶׁהָהַמָּה שֶׁמֶן	SHE-men ham-mish-KHĀH	
	bullock	פַּר	PAR	(Ex. 29:10)
	sin offering	חַטָּאת	khat-TĀT	
	two rams	אֵילִםהָ שְׁנֵי	SHNĒ-hā-ē-LĪM	
	unleavened bread	הַמַּצּוֹת	ham-ma-TSŌT	bread without yeast
3	gather	הַקְהֵל	haq-HĒL	
	congregation	עֵדָה	ē-DĀH	assembly (the heads of all of the tribes)

6 Brought Aaron and his sons (to the lava for washing).

7 "Him": Aaron was dressed different from his sons.

	put upon him	וַיַּחְגֹּר	vay-yakh-GŌR	and he tied, girded
	the coat	כֻּתֹּנֶת	kut-TŌ-net	the tunic
	girdle	בָּאַבְנֵט	bā-av-NĒT	with the sash
9	mitre	תִפְמְצְנ	mits-NE-fet	the turban (see Ex. 28:36-38)
	Holy crown	נֵזֶר	NĒ-zer	of diadem

10 Anointing oil (Ex. 29:7). To anoint is called *masah* from which the name *messiah* comes.

Both things and people were anointed to God:

Jacob anointed a stone.

Furniture was anointed (Ex. 30:26-29).

Aaron was anointed (23-25).

Prophets were also anointed (1 Kings 19:16; 1 Chr. 16:22; Ps. 105-15).

Kings were anointed (1 Sam. 10:1, 16:13, 1 Kings 1:39).

Christ was anointed

Believers are anointed (1 Jn. 2:20).

8	Urim	אוּרִים	ū-RĪM	light
	Thummim	תֻּמִּים	tum-MĪM	perfection

The Urim and Thummim has various conceptions (Ez. 2:63, Neh. 7:65).

1. An oracle attached to the high priest's breast plate through which God's will was made known.

2. Some say that God's name was written and placed-inside the High Priest's breastplate and somehow gave God's approval or disapproval for war etc.

3. Some say that the Urim and Thummim were placed under the High Priest's breastplate as the tables of Law were placed in the Ark of the Covenant (it was placed over the Priest's heart).

Joshua asked counsel for Israel (Num. 27:21), Moses prayed for it (Deut. 33:8, 9), King Saul sought it and was refused of the Lord (1 Sam. 28:6).

Please read Ex. 28:30, Isaiah 61:10, 62:3.

Lessons from the lesson:
- Even leaders must be cleaned up (2, 6).
- God's leaders must let people know who they are speaking for (5, His will carried out).
- God identifies His leader and consecrates him (9).
- Even the Lava, the container to wash dirty hands, was to-be sanctified (11).
- God well dresses His leaders up (spiritually, 7, 13).

Complaints and Cravings

NUMBERS 11:1-6, 10-15

Introduction:

The book of Numbers was written by Moses near the end of his life. It has been given many titles:

---

1   Book of journeying.
2   Book of murmurings.
3   Wayyedabber וַיְדַבֵּר (va-yə-dab-BĒR) "and He said."
4   Arithmoi (according to the Septuagint Greek, meaning 'numbers'). This term is used in the New Testament (Matt. 10:30, Lk. 12:7; Rev. 7:9).
    There were 2 numberings or censuses of the fighting men of Israel (Num. 1:2 @ 603, 550 & Num. 26:2 @ 601, 730).

The book relates the testings of Israel in which they failed miserably. According to Ussher the events therein cover a period of 39 years, from Sinai to Moab. There are 5 divisions:

---

1   The order of the Hose (1:1-10:10).
2   Sinai to Kadesh Barnea (10:11-12:16).
3   At Kadesh Barnea (13:1-19:22).
4   The wilderness wanderings (20:1-33:49).
5   Closing instructions (33:15-36:13, 40 years total 15:1-19:22).

Moses, the writer, lived 120 years and was still in his prime at his death (Deut. 34:7). The key verses in the book are: 10:9 and 10:29.

Israel was at Sinai about 1 year according to Jensen. In 10:11 the guiding cloud was taken up.

Translation, transliteration, interpretation:

v.	English	Hebrew	Pronunciation	Alternative meanings
1	complained	אָנַן	ā-NAN	
	murmur	לוּן	LŪN	

God was displeased and His anger was kindled.

	kindled	חָרָה	khā-RĀH	to burn
	fire	אֵשׁ	ĒSH	

Fire was a symbol of purification (Isaiah 6:6, 7), also of judgement (Lam. 4:11; Lk. 3:9, 16:24; Rev. 4:10-11, 20:14, 15).

2	quenched	שָׁקַע	shā-QA	to abate
3	tabera	תַּבְעֵרָה	tav-ē-RĀH	place of feeding, the burning spot where the fire broke out.

4 Mixed multitude:

This was probably some of the Egyptians who had accompanied them. Possibly a reference to descendants of Bilha & Zilpah (servants of Rachel and Leah, Jacob's wives) (Gen. 30, Ex. 12:38).

The children of Israel wept again, lusting for the eating pleasures of Egypt. They didn't think of the cruelties that they suffered there.

	flesh	בָּשָׂר	bā-SĀR	meat
	fish	דָּגָה	dā-GĀH	
5	freely	חִנָּם	khin-NĀM	

Heb. 5:25, 26: Moses rejected many of the pleasures of Egypt.

6 Mana: this was a test of their obedience (Ex. 16:4), see 7-9 (the dew cleaned the ground where it fell).

God again was displeased and angered at Israel. This time, so was Moses.

Lessons from the lesson:

- Moses' attitude went from intercession to complaining (11).
- Even with all of our needs met thru Jesus, we still often long for the "good old days" rather than the good New Days (5, see 2 Peter 2:20-22; Jn. 6:30-58).
- Chrtstian leaders can get vexed too (10).
- Church members can be like a burden or an affliction (11-15).
- Many leaders and followers, feeling that God is unfair, cease from Church attendance, or giving their offering (as if retaliating against God, 11-15).
- God is big enough, strong enough, and wise enough to handle all of our complaints (16-25), see 1 Peter 5:7; Phil. 4:1-1.

- Before demeaning God's leaders, pray for them; better yet, take a walk in their shoes (see 1 Tim. 5:19; Heb. 13:7, 17).
- Sometimes too much of a good thing is not good (11:18-34).
- Let us make sure that we do not make the journey from an intercessor to a complainer (11-15).

Dissatisfaction and Rebellion

NUMBERS 14:1-12

Introduction:

This is where it all started; Kadesh Barnea. The name means "Holy"; but here it is everything but Holy. This is the same name which the Arabs give for Jerusalem "el khud's".

This was the farthest point reached from Sinai in Israel's direct route to Canaan.

Of the nearly 40 years of wandering in the wilderness, Israel eventually came right back to this place and journeyed to Canaan. Their journey went from Sinai to Kedesh, to Moab (20:1).

This is the place where Miriam died.

Moses had sent the 12 spies into the land, 1 from each tribe, to investigate the land. After their visit, 10 of them brought an evil report (12:32); they invented lies, they left Moses and Aaron and spread rumors among the people. They magnified the giants and minimized themselves (13:33). Nehemiah 9:17 illustrates their sin. They had been away from Sinai only about 2 years and had disclaimed all that God had promised them.

Israel's sin of rebellion:

2	Israel murmured against Moses and Aaron.
	They longed to have died in Egypt, with their stomachs full.
3	Israel blamed God for their trouble.
4	Caleb and Joshua had attempted to still the people with no avail (13:30, 31). Here they were at the point of returning to Egypt, with leadership from another captain.
5	Moses and Aaron fell on their faces; Joshua and Caleb tore their clothes out of regret & shame.
7-9	Caleb and Joshua tried their hand at interceeding in futility.
10	Israel desires to kill Moses and Aaron, charging them with misleading them. It was then that God's glory appeared in the tabernacle before Israel. This was to get their attention, since neither Moses, Aaron, Joshua, nor Cable were able to quell them.
11	Here God in His anger asks Moses a question.

Since God is ominiscient, already knowing, why was this done?

It seems to me that God was giving Moses a chance to recognize His anger and agree with Him. Also, to give Him a chance to interceed for them, and refuse to see himself as better than them, allowing God to use him to make a brand, new nation (greater and stronger).

13-19	Moses again begins to intercede, reminding God of His reputation.
20	God pardoned but brought judgement (to all those over 29 yrs old. 14:29); a day for a year in the wilderness (14:34).
42	Moses warned that God was not with them. They journeyed to the mountain anyway and were killed.
21, 28	God swears to their detriment.
	Ch. 15-19 Redemption.

Lessons from the lesson:

- Focusing on our problems instead of God's promise leads to rejection (14:1-4).
- Sin provokes God to anger (11, 12).
- Some men can very quickly be swayed against God (14:1-4).
- Nothing is as good as God's promise (3).
- Many people are still unwilling to trust God (3).
- Failing to trust God can mislead from the Promised Land (3, 4, Heb. 3:1, 4:10).
- The majority is not always right (14:2); the minority is not always wrong (Num. 14:5, 6).
- If God's people rebel against Him, surly they will rebel against us (9).
- Evil people (so-called Christians) give God a bad reputation (14:15, 16).
- God intervenes for His people (10).
- God is still fulfilling promises (14:8).
- Moses could not answer God's question (11).

Accepting God's Rules for Living

DEUT. 5:1-9A, 11-13, 16-21

Introduction:

Moses, not being permitted to enter into the Promised Land with the children of Israel, is giving His farewell address to them. He is reminding them of their past and prophesying of their future. This is why the writing is called Deuteronomy (repetition).

There is a threefold giving of the law: first, orally, Exodus 20:1-17. Second, on tables of stone, Exodus 24:12-18. Thirdly, after Moses broke the first tables (Exodus 31:18, 32:16-19) God wrote another (Exodus 34:1, 28, 29; Deut. 10:4).

In today's lesson there is a repetition (reminder) of the first giving of the law.

Translation, transliteration, interpretation:

v.	English	Hebrew	Pronunciation	Alternative meanings
1	statutes	חֹק	KHŌQ	precept, edict, ordinance
	judgements	שָׁפַט	shā-FAT	to bring makers to the rule of right
4	face to face	פָּנִים	pa-NĪM	to look on ones face or countenance
	(not to their fathers in Egypt, vs.3)			
5	stood between	עָמַד	ā-MAD	take a stand, come to a stand, succour, defend
6	house of bondage	עָבַד	ā-VAD	to make serve, to keep in bondage
8	graven	χάραγμα	charagma	a mark or stamp, to engrave, to empress]
	likeness	צֶלֶם	TSE-lem	image
11	vain	שָׁוְא	SHĀV	emptiness, nothingness
12	keep	שָׁמַר	shā-MAR	to watch, guard, preserve, retain
16	prolonged	אָרַךְ	ā-RAKH	grow long, continue
	go well	יָטַב	yā-TAV	be good, in the best manner

Lessons from the lesson:

- Knowing God's law is one thing; keeping it is another (1, Jas. 1:22).
- Our God is the God of Covenant; He keeps His word (2).
- Those with whom God makes Covenant are special people (3).

- Face to face infers closeness; God is alive, He communicates with man, He lives in the fire (4).
- Moses was Israel's intercessor; our prayers should be intercessory (5).
- God should not have to remind His saints of His deliverance (6).
- God's government is to be monotheistic and theocratic (7).
- Men often worship gods of their own making (9).
- God's name represents His reputation and should never be used without a good purpose (11).
- The Sabbath Day is a type of the Sabbath Man (Col. 2:16, 17).
- Honoring parents does not guarantee long life, but it sure does not guarantee a short one (16).

Remembering and Celebrating

DEUT. 16:1-8

Introduction:

This sixteenth chapter of Deuteronomy relates 3 of the religious festivals commanded by God to be celebrated by the Hebrews: vs. 1-8, Passover; vs. 9-12, Pentecost; vs. 13-15, Tabernacles. The Passover was to celebrate the freedom from Egyptian bondage which God brought about.

Historical perspective:

Another name for Passover was פֶּסַח (PE-sakh). It was held in the "month of green ears" (March —April).

It was to be held in the month of Abib, which was to be the first month of the religious year.

The month was given a different name (Nisan) after the Babylonian dispersion (Neh. 2:1; Esther 3:7).

Passover also had an agricultural meaning: it was held at the beginning of the barley harvest.

The Jewish calendar is on the lunar year; this is 11 days shorter than the solar year.

It is compensated by inserting an extra month (the second, Adar) 7 times every 19 years (Ex. 12:1).

The Passover meal was to be prepared with unleavened bread; commemorating their hasty departure from Egypt, the leaven or yeast not having time to make the bread rise. Later the leaven became a symbol of evil (1 Cor. 5:7, 8). The residences were to be searched and leaven eradicated. Wherever leaven was found, the family was to be cut off from the nation (Ex. 23:14, 15). Yeast also suggests decay (having no time to rise, Ex. 12:15-20); bread (matzah Ex. 12:18).

The Passover meat was not to be kept to the next day but burned (Ex. 12:10).

The meal was to be eaten in the evening, as it was evening when Pharoah allowed freedom.

The lamb was to be without blemish, hung up and inspected for 3 days (Ex. 12:3, 6).

There was only 1 time when the Passover was not held on the 14th: the Priests were not thoroughly sanctified. ˙

The menu consisted of: egg, green veg, apples, lettuce, horseradish, nuts, wine.

The place for the sacrifice was to be in Jerusalem.

The children's questions were to be answered.

During the feast, Ps. 115-118 is read.

Lessons from the lesson:

- Jesus instituted the Lord's Supper after the Passover meal. They have the same purpose: redemption.
- How soon we forget what God has done for us (3).
- There is to be no leaven of impurity in the Lord's work (1 Cor. 5:7, 8, 3).
- Christians should be in haste to separate from evil (3).
- Freedom is of little value if not used properly (1).
- The seventh day is a day of rest (8).
- All of our children's questions about the Lord's special days should be answered (Ex. 12:26, 27).
- We Christians should remember and celebrate our salvation (3).

The Promise of Life

DEUT. 30:1-10

Introduction:

Today's lesson is about making good choices, and God's rewards that accompany them.

Moses is giving a forecast of the distant future (Deut. 27 and 28 chapters) when Israel would stand on two mountains (Gerizim & Ebal) and choose the blessings of Mt. Gerizim or the curses of Mt. Ebal. God would give them an object lesson: 6 tribes were to stand on Mt. Gerizim (Simeon, Levi, Judah, Issachar, Joseph, Benjamin); and 6 tribes were to stand on the lifeless mountain of Ebal (Reuben, Gad, Asher, Zebulun, Dan, Naphthali). The priests were to stand between them in the valley and facing one then the other with pronouncements of blessings and cursings.

They were told to be faithful (29:1-15) and be blessed or be unfaithful (16-29) and be punished or cursed.

There is the uncertainty as to whether this happened at the return from Babylon, or whether this will happen in modern Israel, during the end time, or the millenium. Also, there is the likelihood that this lesson is applicable to Israel only, although some of the ramifications regarding God's blessings or cursings are lessons for all.

Gerizim was the mountain worshipped on by the Samaritans (Jn. 4:20).

Translation, transliteration, interpretation:

There were 3 sets of 12 stones to be set up and plainly inscribed with God's commandments:

1. In Jordan (Joshua 4:9).
2. In Gilgal (Joshua 4:20).
3. On Mt. Ebal (Deut. 27:4).

v.	English	Hebrew	Pronunciation	Alternative meanings
1	blessing	בְּרָכָה	bə-rā-KHĀH	
	driven	נִדַּח	nā-DAKH	forced away
	called to mind	שׁוּב	SHŪV	

v.	English	Hebrew	Pronunciation	Alternative meanings
2	return	שׁוּב	SHŪV	to turn back
	obey	שָׁמַע	shā-MA	hear, hearken
3	captivity	שְׁבוּת	shə-VŪT	
	gather	קָבַץ	qā-VATS	assemble, collect
	scattered	פוּץ	PŪTS	blow away
		פָּאָה	pā-ĀH	blow away
4	fetch	לָקַח	lā-QAKH	to take or receive (this is called Hebrew parallelism)
5	multiply	רָבָה	rā-VĀH	to make abundant
6	circumcise	מָלַל	mā-LAL	to cut off
	[(alternatively)	περιτέμνω	peritemnō	to cut around (see Acts 7:51; Jer. 9:26; Col. 2:2)]
	these curses	אָלָה	ā-LĀH	execration, detesting, loathing
9	plenteous	יָתַר	yā-TAR	cause to remain over
10	written	כָּתַב	kā-TAV	to write
	keep	שָׁמַר	shā-MAR	take heed, observe

Lessons from the lesson:

- Even before they arrived in the land God forecasted that Israel would be driven out (1, 4).
- Life has its blessings and cursings from God (rewards of living, 1).
- When we drive God away He drives us away (1, 3).
- If we obey the Lord He will do us good (2, 5).
- God can bring sinners back, no matter how far (4).
- Only God can clean an unclean heart (6).
- God often redirects chastisement of His children into punishment on His enemies (7).
- God rejoices in the obedience of His children (9).
- God deserves more than a part of our lives; He deserves and requires all (2, 6, 8, 10).

Joshua: A Leader for the People

JOSH. 1:1-11, 16-17

Introduction:

One of the lessons that we will learn today is that God's work is continuous, and that no one on His program is indispensable. God always has another to take our place.

Translation, transliteration, interpretation:

Joshua's original name was "Hoshea" (Num. 13:8). It was changed by Moses to Jehoshua (Num. 13:16). Jehoshua means, "Salvation is of the Lord" or "Jehovah is salvation." Some say that the name is a prayer, "Jehovah, save from the spies" (evil report). Joshua lived to be 110 years (24:29).

Ussher says that the events in the book cover a period of 26 years.

The key word is "possess," and the key verse is (11:23), "so Joshua took the land."

There are 3 altars mentioned in the book: 1. altar of memorial (4:7), 2. altar of offering (8:30), and 3. the altar of witness (22:34).

The book is called "the book of conquest" 3 attributes of God are prominent: holiness, faithfulness and saving grace.

The book may be divided into 4 parts: preparation, conquest, allotment, consecration.

v.	English	Hebrew	Pronunciation	Alternative meanings
1	After the death of Moses, it's interesting that God didn't allow either of his sons to succeed him, but an unrelated successor named Joshua.			
2	I do give (this was a very big gift, promised of God to their forefathers). It is interesting that even tho it was a gift, they would have to fight for it (and take it).			
3	every place	מָקוֹם	mā-QŌM	place of standing (see 11:24)
5	stand before thee	יצֵּב	yā-TSAV	to set self up
	fail	רָפָה	rā-FĀH	allow to become weak
	forsake	עָזַב	ā-ZAV	fail in war, or forsake after war, abandon
6	strong	חָזַק	khā-ZĀQ	become strong, hard
	good courage	אָמַץ	ā-MATS	be sharp, strong, confirmed

	swear	שָׁבַע	shā-VA	
7	turn	סוּר	SŪR	turn, be turned aside
	prosper	שָׂכַל	sā-KHAL	cause to act wisely
8	this book	סֵפֶר	SĒ-fer	writing (Ps. 119:97)
	mouth	פֶּה	PEH	
	meditate	הָגָה	hā-GĀH	mutter (Ps. 1:2)
9	dismayed	חָתַת	khā-TAT	broken, cast down (Deut.31:23)
11	victuals	צֵדָה	tsē-DĀH	hunting

17 As we harkened unto Moses (there were no questions of God being with Moses except of Korah: Num.16)

Lessons from the lesson:
- Anything that God gives us He will help us keep (5).
- God's promises are sure; we need only to act on them (3, 4) in spite of feelings of inadequacy.
- Knowing that God is with us is encouraging, (5, 6) in any situation.
- God's gifts have to be taken, accepted, received (11).
- Meditating is more than just reading, (7-9) Jas. 1:22.
- Dont let circumstances discourage or cause you to give up (9).
- 3 times God told Joshua to be strong and of good courage (vs. 6, 7, 9).
- God's law should be the standard for His people (8).
- Faith in God should lead to action (10, 11).
- Honoring God means honoring His servants (16, 17).
- Joshua was a type of Christ (a type must be designed by God, futuristic, followed by an antitype):

1	As a leader	Captain of our salvation, Rom. 8:37; 2 Cor. 1:10, 2:14; Heb. 2:10, 11
2	In crossing Jordan	Christians dying with Christ, Rom. 6:6-11; Eph. 2:5, 6; Col. 3:1-3
3	In conquest of Canaan	Christian's victories over enemies, 2 Cor. 10:3-6
4	In His name	Jehoshua - saviour, deliverer.

Commitment to Confront

2 SAM. 12:1-7A, 13-15

Introduction:

There is no sin that is unknown to God. Sin, if it is to be forgiven, must be acknowledged, and repented of to God. Many persons think that they have gotten away or escaped without confessing their sin; still others may use the words "I have sinned" and do not mean them - such was the case with Pharaoh (Ex. 9:27, 10:16), Balaam (Num. 22:34), Saul (1 Sam: 15:24, 30), Judas (Matt. 27:4) - with God, forgiveness follows true confession (1 Jn. 1:9).

Today we study about a sin that was acknowledged, repented of and forgiven.

All of the parables are not in the New Testament; some are in the Old Testament. Of course, parables were the chosen method of our Lord to reveal His heavenly Kingdom. The Greek word for parable is παραβαλλω, *paraballō*, which means to throw alongside, for the purpose of illuminating; it is placing a known along an unknown in order to give light to it. In the lesson today, Nathan, God's prophet during the reign of David, gives a parable to the King.

Keep in mind, a parable is a figure of speech in which a formal comparison is made.

In Matthew's geneology of Jesus there were 4 Gentile women who had sexual sin in their history: Tamar, who committed incest with her father in law. Rahab, who was a harlot, Ruth, who was a Moabite descendant of the incestuous daughter of Lot, Bathsheba, believed to be a Hittite, who committed adultery.

Jesus, the son of man, did come into this world thru sinful men to seek and to save sinners.

Lessons from the lesson:
- When Christians rebuke, it should be done with Divine authorization (1).
- Ignoring sin will not make it go away (1).
- The rebuke of sin should present a picture of guilt (1).
- Your sin will find you out (1, Joshua 7:19).
- God has saints who will not "bite their tongue" with His word (1).
- Evil is easier to see in others than in self (5).
- Even after repentance, consequences must be borne (14).

- Real repentance does not blame others or make excuses (13).
- Confessing to man is one thing; confessing to God is another (13).
- Sin gives God's enemies an occasion to blaspheme and maintain unbelief (14).
- God does take babies out of this world (14).
- Many sinners are tone deaf to God's Holy Spirit.
- Our sin will often affect others as well as ourselves (14).
- How can we effectively condemn other's sins with dirty hands?
- Dont get angry at the messengers (13).
- For David's detailed confession see Ps. 51 & Ps. 32.

Josiah Renewed the Covenant

2 Chr. 34:15, 18-19, 25-27, 29, 31-33

Introduction:

Josiah was 8 yrs old when He became King of Judah. He was the son of Amon, a wicked King. His grandfather was also a wicked King; one having reigned for two yrs, and the other having reigned 55 yrs in Judah. During all this time, the book of the Law had not been followed; as a matter of fact, it had not been seen. Josiah reigned from 640 - 609 B.C. (31 yrs.). Obviously, the prophet or priest had taught him God's Word; his father and grandfather had not done so. Jeremiah had been prophesying five yrs. And Huldah, the prophetess was the wife of a Temple priest.

There is a parallel passage in 2 Kings 22.

During this time, the Temple was in great need of repair; and funds were taken up from the people to accomplish this. The priest was Hilkiah and the scribe was Shaphan.

Josiah, the King, had ordered Shaphan to go to the Temple and find out how much silver had been given for the work. After finding out from the priest, the workers were to be paid, and supplies were to be purchased. In summing up the money, Hilkiah finds an abandoned scroll, which was perhaps a part of Deuteronomy ch. 28, which for 57 yrs had not been read or seen. He takes it to the King and begins to read it to him. Our lesson begins here. Josiah's death came during a war between Egypt and Assyria, in Esdrelon.

Translation, transliteration, interpretation:

v.	English	Hebrew	Pronunciation	Alternative meanings
25	forsaken	רָפָה	rā-FĀH	to be slack, to be loose
	The incense burned probably had been frankincense.			
	provoked	כָּעַס	kā-AS	to be grieved
	poured	נִתַּךְ	nā-TAKH	to flow with force and power as heavy rain
	quenched	כָּבָה	kā-VĀH	to go out, to be extinguished
27	tender	רָכַךְ	rā-KHAKH	soft, gentle, sensitive, yielding
	humble	כָּנַע	kā-NA	bowed down, to subject ones self without conditions

31

	weep	בָּכָה	bā-KHĀH	
	heard	שָׁמַע	shā-MA	to listen, give heed, obey
31	perform	עָשָׂה	ā-SĀH	to make, do, act, execute
32	stand to it	עָמַד	ā-MAD	to take a stand, stand upon
33	abomination	תָּעַב	tā-AV	connected with idolatry, to abhor a deed or practice

There are several words in vs. 31 that should be explained:

commandment	from a word meaning to set up, to give charge.
testimonies	from a word meaning to go back again, to witness, to testify of God's works, power.
statutes	from a word meaning engrave, signifying God's engraving with indelible pen.
precepts	the root here is to oversee, charge, care for, the mandate of God commanding our obedience.
word	the root means to reveal, to bring to light as an utterance which reveals the speakers mind. There is a clear shining of the sure word of prophecy.
law	the root is to project as an arrow from a bow; hence to point out or teach rendered shot signifying the direction of God in pointing out the rule of His will.
judgement	to give a finding which is just and right. The root here means to set upright. It denotes God's verdict. Translated ordinance.

Most of these words are written in Psalms 19:7-9 (We are thankful to Dr. F. E. Marsch for this etymology).

Lessons from the lesson:
- Before punishing, God showed the people His Law, so they would know why they would be punished (34:15, 25).
- Children whose parents neglect God do not have much alternative (25).
- Disregard of God's Word provokes Him to anger (25).
- God's wrath can only be quenched by repentance and obedience (25).
- We must read God's Word to know our responsibilities (18).
- Many godly children are descendants from ungodly homes (18).
- Children of God recognize His word when they hear it read (19).

- God's Word is often discarded as trash (15).
- There are times when the Bible should be read aloud (2 Kings 23:2, 2 Chr. 34:30).
- Humility is rare among leaders today (27).
- There are still a few tenderhearted saints left in the world today (27).
- God will not say well done to the undone (27).
- If God's Word is written in our hearts in can never be lost (15).
- Whenever we measure ourselves it should be against God's commandments (31).
- Josiah made a Covenant to keep God's Covenant (31).
- God's house should be kept in good repair (2 Chr. 34:8, 2 Kings 22:5).
- God's people should be able to go to His prophet for directions (26).

Ezra: A Priest for the People
EZRA 9:5-11, 15

Introduction:

Our lesson today deals with Ezra, who was a priest and a scribe (7:6, 21). Ezra was in a second deportation of Israel from Persia. He was prominent at a very critical time in Israel. After arriving in Israel (458 B.C.) he made vast reforms upon seeing the sinful condition of the people. In his prayer for Israel, he identifies with them, although he was not involved in their sins. He uses 26 plural pronouns of the 1st person.

History:

Ezra's name עֶזְרָא means "God helps" and is believed to be derived from Azariah. In the Greek language the name is Esdras. In the book (7:1-21) we read of his genealogy. Ezra was commissioned by the Persian King Artaxerxes I to return to his home land and reorganize the area in and around Jerusalem. The Temple had been rebuilt by Zerubbabel before he arrived. Ezra is the author of the book that bears his name. The Hebrews combined his book with Nehemiah making one book, until much later single copies were found which divided them into single books. The book of Ezra was placed in the third division (the hagiographa) with Daniel and Nehemiah, before Chronicles. Abarbanel, in his commentary on Samuel, asserts Ezra to be a continuation of Chronicles, because it begins with "and"; Chronicles ending with 2 verses which are at the beginning of Ezra.

Nehemiah is said to have completed Ezra's book after his death, as Joshua completed Moses' book after his death. Ezra is said to have lived to be 120 years (by tradition); a portion of Ezra's writing is called "the Psalm of Ezra" (7:27, 28).

Several passages in Ezra are completed by Nehemiah.

Ezra's writing style is different from Haggai or Zechariah and is more like Malachi's.

There are many Aramaisms in his vocabulary (4:8, 6:18, 7:12-26).

Judea became a Persian province (530-334).

In Ezra's reforms, the Torah was removed from the exclusive possession of the priests to the possession of the nation as a whole.

Israel, falling into sin again, might expect another chastening from God. The priests were the chief offenders. Haggai, Zechariah, and Malachi were very helpful during this era.

Translation, transliteration, interpretation:

v.	English	Hebrew	Pronunciation	Alternative meanings
5	During the evening sacrifice (Deut. 7:1-5.)			

Ezra expressed his heaviness and grief over the mixed marriages of the Hebrews. (Ex. 34:11-16) here is an irony, sacrifice in the midst of sinful living without repentance.

Here is the best posture of prayer. Upon knees with spread out hands unto the Lord.

	English	Hebrew	Pronunciation	Alternative meanings
	heaviness	תַּעֲנִית	ta-ă-NĪT	affliction, humiliation

This condition was very similar to the sins of Solomon (1 Kings 11:1-11, Judges 3:5, 6).

	English	Hebrew	Pronunciation	Alternative meanings
	blush	כָּלַם	kā-LAM	accompanies shame, pain, distress
6	ashamed	בֹּשֶׁת	BŌ-shet	to become pale
	over our head	לְמַעְלָה	lə-MA-lāh	above (here is the allusion of drowning) Ps. 38:5
	lift up my face	רום	RŪM	make high

his face is hidden in shame.

	English	Hebrew	Pronunciation	Alternative meanings
	grown up into the heavens	גִּדֵּל	gā-DAL	become great
7	confusion of face, see vs. 6 (Daniel 9:7; 2 Chr. 32:21) shame faced			
8	a little space	רֶגַע	RE-ga	a moment
	grace	תְּחִנָּה	tə-khin-NĀH	supplication for grace
	nail	יָתֵד	yā-TĒD	peg (as to hold down a tent in soil), see Isaiah 54:2
	and now	וְעַתָּה	və-at-TĀH	

This all began 80 yrs earlier with Zerubbabel (in comparison with centuries of sin it is a brief moment).

	English	Hebrew	Pronunciation	Alternative meanings
	remnant	שְׁאָר	shə-ĀR	the rest,

This term was used by Joseph in interpreting his presence in Egypt.

	English	Hebrew	Pronunciation	Alternative meanings
	reviving	מִחְיָה	mikh-YĀH	preservation
9	bondmen	עֶבֶד	E-ved	slave, servant

They are still subject to Persian rule.

	English	Hebrew	Pronunciation	Alternative meanings
	wall	גָּדֵר	gā-DĒR	hedge, fence
10	after this	שׁוּב	SHŪV	turn back

Lessons from the lesson:

- Living in sin leads to misery (6, 7).
- Unconfessed sin is an offence to God (6, 7).

- Even in the best times we should maintain a sense of our undeserved standing before God (9).
- Often, iniquities lead out of control (7).
- Prayer involves a relationship with God (5-15).
- If one has married into heathen practices which tempt against God, ending the marriage is critical (10:3).
- God's punishment is much less than we deserve (9:13).

Following a Visionary Leader

NEH. 2:1-8, 11, 17-18

Introduction:

All leaders are not visionary. This kind of leader has been given a vision by God; and he follows it, leading God's people in the vision.

Nehem-yah's name means "the comfort of Jehovah." He was born in exile, in a godly home. And at a young age was appointed cup bearer to the Persian King Artaxerxes. He was in the third contingent of exiles; and he had a sensitive ear to God (2:12, 7:5). Early writers like Origen called his book the second book of Ezra (who spoke of the wall; Ezra 9:9).

Nehemiah נְחֶמְיָה records a list of Jewish families that were in the return (7:5-73).

This list is almost identical with Ezra's list (Ezra 2:1-70).

12 years after Ezra's book closes, Nehemiah's begins (Ezra 7:8, 10:16-17, Neh. 1:1, 2:1); then he records the events of the next 20 years.

The first return was under Zerubbabel (536) the second return was under Ezra (458) and the third return was under Nehemiah (445). Malachi would come along around 435.

Nehemiah was appointed governor of Judah by the King, a position which he held for 12 yrs.

He had much opposition both from within and from without (4:1-23, 5:1-19, 6:1-14). The wall was finally finished in 52 days (6:15, 7:73).

The following list shows the chronology of the reigns of the Persian Kings:

Cyrus	550 B.C.
Cambyses	530 B.C.
Smerdis	520 B.C.
Darius I	516 B.C.
Xerxes	486 B.C.
Artaxerxes Longimanus	464 B.C. The 20th year of his reign would make the time of Nehemiah's release around 444 B.C.

37

Translation, transliteration, interpretation:

v.	English	Hebrew	Pronunciation	Alternative meanings
1	sad	רָעַע	rā-A	to make to be evil
2	countenance	פָּנִים	pā-NĪM	the face
	sick	חָלָה	khā-LĀH	diseased, weak
	sorrow of heart	רֹע	RŌA	evil, badness
	sore	מְאֹד	mə-ŌD	exceedingly
	afraid	יָרֵא	yā-RĒ	reverence, fear
3	waste	בָּתָה	bā-TĀH	desolation
	consumed	אָכַל	ā-KHAL	to be eaten, used up.
4	request	בַּקֵשׁ	biq-QĒSH	to seek, to pray
5	build	בָּנָה	bā-NĀH	to build up
6	set a time	נָתַן	nā-TAN	to give
7	letters	תרְאָג	ig-GE-ret	
	convey	עָבַר	ā-VAR	cause to pass over
8	appertained	היא	yā-ĀH	to be becoming
	granted	נָתַן	nā-TAN	to give

The Euphrates river was the dividing line.

The King's Cavalry accompanied Nehemiah.

Nehemiah waited 3 days before beginning, as also did Ezra when he came (Ezra 8:32).

Application:

- The results of God's judgement should make the recipients sad (2).
- God often works thru secular authorities (4).
- Prayer changes people (4).
- When God's house lies in waste and in shambles, He is dishonored and so are His people (3).
- All things do work together for good to those who love the Lord (Rom. 8:28, 2:6).
- Sometimes God's people must work in secret (2:12-16).
- God's people work the night shift also (2:12-16).
- God is moving even when the worldly are having a good time (Dan. 5:1-5; Neh. 2:1).
- The Lord's work should never stop (6:2).
- A visionary leader will encourage others (18).
- Where there is no vision the people perish (Prov. 29:18).
- Much can be accomplished when God's people work together (6:15).

- When we relate to others what God has done and is doing, they will be excited too (18).
- What a shame that God's house has to be guarded (7:1).
- God's hand is good (2:8).

Finishing the Task

Neh. 4:1-13, 6-9, 13-15, 6:15

Introduction:

I am amazed at the many devices which the adversaries of the Lord and His people use in order to stop or defer His work. It infers that God's work offends many, who rebel against Him. The lesson here for the saints is that we will face opposition from many directions, both from the outside and from the inside.

Characters in the lesson:

San-bal'lat	A Moabite of Horonaim (2:9, 19, 13:28) who held a military command in Samaria for Artaxerxes. His daughter married one of priest Eliashib's grandsons. He was allied with Tobiah. Nehemiah had expelled the Priest (13:28).
Tobiah	An Ammonite whose relatives returned from Babylon with Zerubbabel. It is said he was unable to prove his connection with Israel (Ezra 2:60; Neh. 7:62, 6:16-19).
Geshem	An Arabian (2:19, 4:7-9, 6:1, 2, 6). An inhabitant of Arabia, maybe a tribal chief.

The Nations:

Moab and Ammon had been hateful toward Israel, when they first entered Caanan. The Ammonites' territory near the wall was to the east. San-bal'lat's teritory near the wall was to the north. The Arabian's territory was to the south.

The Ashdodites' territory was to the west (possible descendents from Ashdod, one of five capital cities of the Philistines).

History:

Nehemiah and the builders of the wall were surrounded by their enemies who opposed the rebuilding of the wall.

Shemaiah, a false prophet had been hired by the opposition to lure Nehemiah (6:10-14), but God was with him and gave him perception.

Five times Nehemiah had been invited to come down from the wall (6:4).

There was a false report made against Nehemiah and the builders (6:5-8), Ez. 4:13.

There was also inside opposition (ch. 5) the outside enemies were planning to kill them (4:11).

Translation, transliteration, interpretation:

v.	English	Hebrew	Pronunciation	Alternative meanings
1	indignation	כַּעַס	KA-as	anger, sadness
	mocked	לָעַג	lā-AG	scorn
	confusion	תּוֹעָה	tō-ĀH	to wander, stray, bewilderment
8	conspired	קָשַׁר	qā-SHAR	to bind
10	decayed	כָּשַׁל	kā-SHAL	ready to fall, feeble, stumbling
4:13	weapon	הַשֶּׁלַח	has-SHĀ-lakh	missile, javelin

- Nehemiah and the builders prayed many times during their troubles, so should we. Their prayer was imprecatory (revenge on their enemy).
- Odds may be against us, but they are not against God.
- Once you pray, don't stop. Prayer should be continual (4:5, 9).
- Prayer doesn't mean stop watching (9).
- In spite of prayer, things may seem to get worse (8).
- We are surrounded by opposition; without God's help we would be swallowed up (Ps. 46).
- Faith in God must be tested.
- When surrounded by the opposers use the trumpet (4:20).
- God's not given us the spirit of fear, but of power and of a sound mind (2 Tim. 1:7).
- Nehemiah didn't have a big army but God is the Lord of Hosts.
- We should never forget that God is awsome and full of terror (14).
- Today we deal with the same type of Satanic pests as Nehemiah.
- Don't stop until you have finished, שָׁלֵם (shā-LĒM), completed the job (6:15).
- Hanani (who had originally informed Nehemiah of the bad condition of the walls) was rewarded (7:2).
- If the devil doesn't stop you he will hinder you.

<h1>*Restored and Renewed*</h1>

NEH. 8:1-3, 5-6, 13-14, 17-18

Introduction:

The term 'restore' has several meanings:

1	חָיָה	khā-YĀH	to make alive again (2 Kings 8:1, 5)
2	עָלָה	ā-LĀH	to heal or be healed (Jer. 30:17, 'I will heal thee of thy wound...')
3	שׁוּב	SHŪV	to turn back (Ps. 23:3, 'Thou restoreth my soul.') (Gen. 20:7)
4	שָׁלֵם	shā-LĒM	to make whole or complete (Joel 2:25, 'I will restore to you the years...')
5	ἀποκαθίστημι	apokathistēmi	to give back (Matt. 17:11, 'Elias shall truly come and restore...')

The term 'renew' has several meanings:

1	חָדַשׁ	khā-DASH	to repair (Ps. 51:10, 'Create in me...renew a right spirit...')
2	חָלַף	khā-LAF	to pass on, to change (Isaiah 40:31, 'They that wait...renew')
3	ἀνακαινίζω	anakainizō	to make new again (Heb. 6:6)

The seventh Jewish month was Tishri. This month held several special days: Feast of Trumpets, the Day of Atonement, and the Feast of Tabernacles.

Without having rebuilt the walls around the city, it would have been very difficult; with much insecurity, for the Jews to have held these Holy days. This was the time of the Feast of Trumpets (Lev. 23:23, 24).

Moses had directed the people, before he died, to gather, every 7 years and read God's Word (Deut. 31:9-13).

History:

1) As one man, into the street (see Ezra 3:1).

There was unity here in their worship.

The Water Gate: this gate was on the east side of the city, near the Gihon spring, where King Solomon was anointed (1 Kings 1:33, 38, 45, Neh. 3:26).

Book of the Law of Moses: this was the Torah. The people had a great desire to hear the word of the Lord during this special occasion.

Here Ezra is described as a scribe; later he would be described as a priest (Ezra 7:21).

2) The people heard God's Word with understanding.

3) Morning til mid-day, the people listened to the reading.

5) Above the people, Ezra was on a platform (a pulpit) with 13 assistants (vs. 4). All the people stood up, giving credence to God's Word.

6) Amen, this means, so be it, I agree, certainly, etc. Jesus is God's amen.

9) The people wept; but were admonished not to do so but be joyful (9-12). Not a time for fasting.

Tirshatha, spiritual leader (Ezra 2:63). Nehemiah was the secular leader.

13) The next day, the people must have left and returned.

14) They found written in the law regarding the Feast of Tabernacles (Lev. 23:23-43).

15-16) The people went to the Mount of Olives and cut down trees for booths: olive trees, pine, myrtle and palm; never with this kind of enthusiasm and joy.

17) There was great gladness (Deut. 16:14).

There were three types of responses: intellectual (vs. 1-8), emotional (vs. 9-12), volitional (13-18).

Lessons from the lesson:
- God's Word must be taken seriously if His people are to receive strength.
- Our gathering to the Lord should be unified, as one man (1).
- There is no harm in coming outside of the building and gathering in the street for worship (1).
- When God's people hunger for His word they need a skilled, well trained, dedicated teacher (1).
- The Bible should be read with understanding (2).
- The people of God should find a Church where His Word is proclaimed and explained (2).
- To worship God from morning til noon is not too long (3).
- It is a blessing to have a personal copy of God's Word (2).
- Amen, expresses our agreement with God's Word (6).
- Hands up and heads bowed is a good worship posture (6).
- There should be more Vacation Bible school and week day Bible study (18).
- There should be great gladness today in hearing God's Word (17).
- There are many wonderful things to be found in God's Word (14).
- Scripture is one medium of God's world-wide revelation.

Risky Commitments

ESTHER 4:1-3, 9-17

Introduction:

We have before us a lesson in God's providence, of which we will be more specific later.

The book of Esther is the last of the 5 Megilloth (scrolls). In the Hebrew Canon, the books of "Song of Solomon," "Ruth," "Lamentations" and "Ecclesiastes" have been listed in prior order.

These books are called the "Kethubim" or the "Hagiographa" (writings). In the Hebrew canon, the order is the Torah, the Writings, then the Prophets.

The approximate dates of the Kings of Persia are:

Cyrus 550-536, Cambyses 530-521, Smerdis, Darius 1st 521-486, Xerxes 486-464, Artaxerxes 1st 464-42:

Another name for Esther (אֶסְתֵּר) was Hadassah. She and her cousin Mordecai were of the tribe of Benjamin. Esther's father was Abihail. Both he and her mother had died. Mordecai looked after her.

According to the Scriptural reading:

2:17	Esther is selected Queen.
2:10	Mordecai cautions her not to reveal her kindred.
2:21-23	Mordecai uncovers a plot to kill the King.
3:1	Haman is promoted.
3:2	Mordecai refuses to bow to him.
3:8, 9	Haman persuades the King to issue a decree to kill all of the Jews.
3:13	The date is set for the killing (the last month in the year, adar).
4:1	Mordecai hears the news and begins to mourn in sack cloth.
4:4	The Queen hears and sends him a change of clothes.
4:7, 8	Mordecai sends evidence to the Queen and charges her to speak to the King.
4:11	Esther informs Mordecai of the danger in going before the King.
4:14	Mordecai warns her of the danger to the Jews.
4:15	Esther proclaims a 3 day fast.

5:1	The King admits Esther in his presence. She invites the King and Haman to a banquet.
5:14	Haman's wife advises him to make a gallow to hang Mordecai on.
6:1	The King can not sleep. Reads records of the Chronicles, discovering Mordecai's good deed.
6:6	Haman, having come to the King to get permission to hang Mordecai, is spoken to first by the King: "what is to be done for the man that the King desires to honor?" Haman, thinking that the King is speaking about him, suggests an elaborate honoring plan.
6:10	The King tells Haman to do it for Mordecai.
6:13	Haman's wife now directs him to relent because of providence.
6:14	The King sends for Haman to go to Esther's banquet.
7:4	Esther tells the King of Haman's plot.
7:7	The King is angry and goes out of the room.
7:8	When he returns he finds Haman on the Queen's bed (begging for his life).
7:10	Haman is ordered to be hung on his own gallows which he fixed for Mordecai.
8:5	Esther requests a reversal of the King's edict.
9:20-22	Mordecai begins the feast of Purim.

A lesson in providence:

Providence is that continuous agency of God by which He makes all of the events of the physical and moral universe fulfill the original design with which He created it.

Rom. 8:28: And we know that all things work together for good to them that love God, to them who are the called according to His purpose.

We observe God's providence in action in at least nine ways:

Esther, being favored by the King, replaces Vashti.

Mordecai observing a plot to kill the King.

The King couldn't sleep and reads the Chronicle.

Mordecai hears of the plot to kill the Jews.

The King admits Esther into his presence.

The King favors Mordecai.

Haman's wife recognizes God's providence.

Haman mistakenly thinks that the King is planing to honor him again.

The King enters and finds Haman having fallen on Esther's bed.

Lessons from the lesson:

- Some people get the "big head" when they are promoted (3:2, 5).
- God's people are being watched (3:3, 5).
- Prayer and fasting is always in order. It is the antidote for perilous times (4:1).
- Through prayer and fasting we are led to the comfort of God's plan for us (4:1).
- Sometimes it seems like there is no way out (4:14).
- God raises men up, and He casts men down (4:13, 14).
- "A time such as this" is our time (4:14).
- We may be called upon by God to do some risky things for His glory (4:9-11).
- Trouble will not go away by doing nothing; it could get worse (4:12, 13).
- If we don't honor God, some one else is waiting to take our place (4:14).
- Servants of God will be tested (4:8, 16).
- Pur is the Persian word for lots.

The Foreshadowing of Messiah's Birth

ISAIAH 7:13-17; LK. 1:30-38

Introduction:

Jesus is the χριστος (christos, Greek), and the מָשִׁיחַ (Hebrew language), meaning 'the anointed one of God,' who would deliver Israel and the world.

Today's lesson asserts this fact from both the Old and New Testaments.

In order to obtain clarity, we must read: Isaiah 7:1, 2, 10, 11-16; 2 Kings 16, 2 Chr. 28.

Pekah is King of the Northern Kingdom of Israel, and Rezin is King of Syria. They have made an alliance to attack Ahaz and the Southern Kingdom. Their effort was not successful. Meanwhile King Ahaz being fearful removes some of the gold and silver from the Temple to pay the King of Assyria to help him (2 Ki. 16:7, 8). Ahaz is a wicked King but Isaiah delivers a message from God that God would defend his Kingdom, and that he should trust God and ask Him for a sign of assurance. Ahaz, being stubborn, having made an alliance with the King of Assyria, refuses the offer of a sign; but God gives the sign anyway.

The sign was, that a virgin, during the reign of Kings Rezin and Pekah, would conceive and bear a son, and that God thru Him would be with the Southern Kingdom. There is much speculation as to the meaning of this sign. Some say that this son was the son of Isaiah, others that He was the son of Hezekiah. Whomever this son was then, the sign has a double fulfillment. The ultimate fulfillment was that the virgin would be Mary and the son would be Jesus the Christ, Son of God.

Translation, transliteration, interpretation:

v.	English	Hebrew	Pronunciation	Alternative meanings
Isaiah 7:13	weary	לָאָה	lā-ĀH	to press, make heavy, be fatigued, to vex, become tired, despondant
7:14	virgin	עַלְמָה	al-MĀH	a chaste, unmarried, young woman
		בְּתוּלָה	bə-tū-LĀH	separation
	Immanuel	עִמָּנוּ אֵל	im-MĀ-nū = with us + ĒL= God: (God with us)	
7:15	butter	חֶמְאָה	khem-ĀH	
	honey	דְּבַשׁ	də-VASH	debash

These two food items may have been indicative of difficult times.

17:15	evil	רַע	RA	iniquity, vanity, worthlessness
7:15	good,	טוֹב	TŌV	
7:16	abhor	קוּץ	QŪTS	
	forsaken	עָזַב	ā-ZAV	to be left, cease, reject, leave, abandon (of both her Kings)

v.	English	Greek	Transliterated	Alternative meanings
Luke 1:30	favour	χάριν	charin (chairō)	grace, delight in, gladness
1:31	conceive	συλλήμψῃ	sullēmpsē (sullambanō)	seize, become pregnant
1:32	great	μέγας	megas	
	throne	θρόνον	thronon	
1:35	come upon	ἐπελεύσεται	epeleusetai	overtake, happen to unexpectedly, (eperchomai)
	overshadow	ἐπικιάσει	episkiasei	a figure of a cloud coming upon her as the shadow of Peter (Acts 5:15)

Lessons from the lesson:
- In describing Egypt and Assyria, God calls one a "fly" and the other a "bee" (7:18, 19).
- Refusing to accept God's signs doesn't keep God from sending them (7:13).
- It is dangerous to try God's patience (7:13).
- A prophecy can have a near fulfillment, and a far fulfillment (7:14, Lk. 1:30).
- God specializes in difficult cases (Lk. 1:31).
- God's people are given diets for difficult times (Isaiah 7:15).
- Finding favour with God should be the universal goal of man (1:30).
- There are 2 miracles in the story of Jesus:
- Pregnancy without a man (Lk. 1:34, 35).
- Pregnancy in old age (Lk. 1:36).
- Proper response to God incurs His favour (Lk. 1:1, 38).
- With God nothing is impossible (Lk. 1:37).
- Isaiah's two sons' names were:
- Maher-shalal-hash-baz (meaning, speed to the spoil) 8:3, 4.
- Shear-jashub (meaning, a remnant shall return) 7:3.

New Leadership

EZE. 34:23-31

Introduction:

Today we will study about sheep and shepherd; the restoration of Israel from captivity; the one-thousand year reign of Christ; some of the visions of the prophet Ezekiel.

Let us consider some of the visions of Ezekiel first. Many of them were symbolical-typical:

4:4, 5	He was to lay on His left side when he went to bed, for 390 days, and then lay on his right side for 40 days, symbolizing Israel and Judah's sins, totaling 430 years spent in Egypt.
4:9-17	He was to prepare human excrement for his meal (animal dung was substituted). This would illustrate the coming scarcity of food because of Israel's sin.'
5:1-4	He was to shave his head and scatter 1/3 to the wind, 1/3 to be burned, and 1/3 to be cut through with the sword. Illustrating Israel's scattering and death by fire & sword.
4:1-3	He was commanded to draw on a tile a city under siege, symbolizing Judah under siege.
10:18	The Glory Cloud of the Lord departed from the Temple.
43:2	The Glory Cloud of the Lord returned.
6:11	Ezekiel was to clap his hands and stamp his feet to get Israel's attention.
12:1-16	In another vision he was to dig a hole in the city wall and carry scant baggage; This would show a future hurried departure from their homes, desperation to leave, with covered faces indicating the coming blindness of King Zedikiah (2 Kings 25:1-7).
12:17-20	He was to tremble and ration his water as though it was his last.
21:9-17	He would slash a gleaming sword in the air while beating himself on the thigh.
21:18-22	He would draw a map showing two routs for the King of Babylon's approach to Jerusalem and Rabbath Ammon.

24:1-14	He was to prepare a pot full of good food, then throw it out, leaving the empty pot on the fire to burn and rust. This also made reference to Israel's captivity for sin.
36:1-7	Israel would be restored, and the Gentiles who sneered at them would be shamed.
36:20-23	God's great name would be exonerated (through the restoration, 37:1-4).
34:23	During the Millennium David metaphorically would be God's undershepherd and His Kingdom would be established (Christ being the Good Shepherd, Chief Shepherd, Great Shepherd: Jn. 10:11-15, 27-29; Heb. 13:20-21; 1 Pe. 5:4).

Isaiah 11: the new Millenial Kingdom would be set up.

The pre Millenialists contend that Christ will return before the Millennium (Rev. 20) the post Millenialists believe that Christ will not return until after the Millennium. The Amillennialists say that there will be no 1000 year reign (only in the hearts of the believers).

For references to the future Millennial reign of Christ see Isaiah 9:7, 42:4-7, 59:16-21, 11:3-5, 49:1-12, 32:1, 33:22.

The Davidic Covenant was made to David, 2 Sam. 7:16, 8-17.

David was a type of Christ who would sit on His throne (Luke 1:31-33; Acts 2:29-32, 15:14-17, 34:25-28; Hos. 3:5; Jer. 30:9; Ezekiel 37:24).

Ezekiel 34:1-22: read this background before reading the lesson.

Lessons from the lesson:
- God has a plan; and it will prevail (23).
- God chooses to call His followers sheep (23).
- No one is outside of God's Decree (25, 26).
- God's chastisement is only temporary (29, Ps. 103:8, 9).
- He chastens His people but judges His enemy.
- The flock of God will be one-fold (34:31).
- The time will come when all will know the Lord (Ex. 6:7; Ezekiel 34:30).
- God will exonerate His Great Name, and the shame of the heathen will be gone (Lev. 26:20, 26; Hos. 2:8, 9; Hag. 1:5, 6).
- God Himself gives us assurance (24, Isaiah 11:1; Jer. 23:5).
- The wild animals will not be wild; their appetites will be changed (34:28, Isaiah 11:6, 7).
- God's unbroken Covenant of peace will unite His people (25, Lev. 26:6-8; Ezekiel 3:1-13).

- The bands of the enemy will not be strong enough to hold God's people (27).
- God is still giving deliverance from oppressors (27).
- Amos says that the plowman will overtake the reaper (29, Amos 9:13).
- Showers of blessing will fall (26).
- God's blessings may seem too good to be true but they are (24).
- Others will see God's blessings falling on His people and seek them (Zech. 8:20-23).
- The Son of David will feed God's people with good food (not junk food, 23).

A New Spirit Within

EZE. 36:22-32

Introduction:

God has a spotless reputation, verified by His name. He is concerned about it being tarnished, giving the world the wrong impression of Himself. This is done when His chosen ones live contrary to, and in non-conformity with His Character, Will and Word. This is the main lesson in the text that is before us today.

Translation, transliteration, interpretation:

v.	English	Hebrew	Pronunciation	Alternative meanings
22	Holy	קָדוֹשׁ	qā-DŌSH	sanctity, separate, set apart
	name	שֵׁם	SHĒM	renown, reputation, memory
	profane	חָלַל	khā-LAL	to pollute, make common
23	great	גָּדוֹל	gā-DŌL	in high esteem
	sanctified	קָדֵשׁ	qā-DASH	be Holy
25	sprinkle	זָרַק	zā-RAQ	to wash, cleanse
	filthiness	טֻמְאָה	tum-ĀH	uncleanness
	idols	לִּימוֹלִג	gil-lū-LĪM	that which are rolled about. Dung pellets
26	new	חָדָשׁ	khā-DĀSH	recent, fresh
27	statutes	חֹק	KHŌQ	decreed limit, portion
	judgements	מִשְׁפָּט	mish-PĀT	judicial verdict, rights
29	save	יָשַׁע	yā-SHA	give ease
	uncleanness	טֻמְאָה	tum-ĀH	defilement
	corn	דָּגָן	dā-GĀN	grain
30	reproach	חֶרְפָּה	kher-PĀH	disgrace, shame, revile
31	iniquities	עָוֺן	ā-VŌN	perversity
	abominations	תּוֹעֵבָה	tō-ē-VĀH	
32	ashamed	בּוֹשׁ	BŌSH	become pale
	confounded	כָּלַם	kā-LAM	to put to shame

Lessons from the lesson:

- God's name is Holy (22).
- We who have received God's grace can disgrace Him (22).
- God is concerned about His reputation (22).
- Our evil deeds and misdeeds give God a bad name among the heathen (22).
- Those who are called Christians carry God's Holy Name with them everywhere they go (23).
- The heathen figured that God could not prevent the Hebrews from being exiled; but God was the one who was chastening them by expulsion.
- The heathen also believed that the Hebrews' God could not deliver them from captivity; but it was God who had set the time of their expulsion and their release (24).
- God's ability to keep His word was being questioned and continues to be questioned (22).
- Only God can clean filthy lives (25).
- The sprinkling with water was a form of the Mosiac purification (25), Num. 19:11, 12, 17-19.
- God knows how to clean His people up (25).
- The redeemed can never forget where God has brought them from (31).
- God's reputation demanded Israel's punishment; but it also demanded their restoration (31).
- God's reputation is still at stake (22).
- Many hearts are made of "stone" (26).
- Jeremiah had already spoken of a new Covenant (31:31-14).
- Speaking of the Messianic Age, see: Eze. 37:14, 39:29.

A Vision of New Life

EZE. 37:1-14

Introduction:

In today's lesson, Ezekiel is having yet another vision. This one is also about revival, reunion and restoration. His name means "God strengthens." God made him hard hearted in order to resist rebellious Israel (3:8, 9). In the first year of Israel's deportation, Daniel was in the group taken to Babylon; 8 years later, Ezekiel was in the second deportation (2 Kings 24:10-17; some exiles were killed trying to escape; some were imprisoned, and some were allowed to have settlements Jer. 29:1-7; Ez. 1:2, 33:21). Many Jews could not tell their heritage (Ezra 2:59; Neh. 7:61). Many elders came to Ezekiel for instruction and inspiration (8:1, 14:1, 20:1).

It is interesting to know the themes of the major prophets: Isaiah (Salvation of the Lord), Jeremiah (Judgement of the Lord), Daniel (Kingdom of the Lord), Ezekiel (sovereignty of the Lord).

It is also interesting to know that Ezekiel mentions Daniel 3 times in the book (14:14, 20, 28:3); Daniel mentions Jeremiah once (Dan. 9:2).

In the book we will find Ezekiel repeating "the Word of the Lord came to me" some 49 times; "the hand of the Lord was upon me" some 7 times (1:3; 3:14, 22; 8:1; 33:22; 37:1; 40:1); "Lord God" some 200 times. God expresses "they shall know" some 70 times in the Book.

Those Israelites who were serious about His visions would ask for their meaning (12:9, 24:19, 37:18).

Translation, transliteration, interpretation:

v.	English	Hebrew	Pronunciation	Alternative meanings
1	carried	אצי	yā-TSĀ	to bring forth, to carry forth.
	spirit	רוח	RŪAKH	this is the same word for wind, breath
	set (me down)	נוח	NŪAKH	cause to rest
	full	מְלֵא	mā-LĒ	fullness, abundance
2	very dry	יָבֵשׁ	yā-VĒSH	dry, dried up

(The bones were laying there as if having been from a fight or battle).

54

Ezekiel was excited as he uses the term "many" and "very dry." He was careful not to touch the bones because of defilement (Lev. 21:1; Num. 19:11).

3   This was an indication of their conception that all hope was gone (11).
     God's question to Ezekiel was an illustration that Israel was beyond human power of restoration.
     Talking to the bones was, figuratively, personification.

6   sinews   גִּיד   GĪD   tendon, nerves
     lay   נָתַן   nā-TAN   to give

7   Noise (commotion) the bones not only moved, but each bone went to its place in its body. Shaking (forming, shaking).

8   bones   עֶצֶם   E-tsem
     The term "prophecy" is in these verses some 7 times.

9   slain   חָרַג   hā-RAG   slaughter
     #4 (earth): this is a symbol of God's universal life, giving Spirit.

10   stood up   קוּם   QŪM   to place one's self
     They stood on their feet. This is a type; Jesus will raise (Jn. 5:21, 24-26, 28, 29) men and women from the dead.
     exceeding great מְאֹד   mə-ŌD   very much great

11   Here God interprets the vision for Ezekiel.
     bones are dried יָבֵשׁ   yā-VĒSH
     hope lost   קָוֶה   qā-VĀH
     cut off   גָזַר   gā-ZAR   separate, divide, perish, fail

12   open   פָּתַח   pā-TAKH   draw out
     graves   שְׁאוֹל   shə-ŌL   receptacle for the dead
     They were bones atop of the ground; now they are corpses in graves.

13   bring you   בּוֹא   BŌ   cause to come in, bring in
     ye shall know   יָדַע   yā-DA   to perceive, to understand
     I have spoken it אָמַר   ā-MAR   to say
     performed   עָשָׂה   ā-SĀH   to make, to do, to act
                                              (see Jeremiah 33:14-16)

Lessons from the lesson:
   •   A resurrection is only possible by God thru His word (10).
   •   Bones are only bones without the breath of God (8, Gen. 2:7).
   •   The resurrection is not just a promise but God's guarantee (6).
   •   God's Word has power thru our witness (7, 9, 10).

- God's miracles all call attention to Himself (7, 10).
- Death may be man's enemy but God's servant (3, 11).
- God's hand is upon His servants today (37:1).
- Here is a distinction between what God knows and what man knows (3).
- Nothing is so helpless that God can't fix it (11, 12, Matt. 19:26).

Holding to Your Convictions

DANIEL 1:8-20

Introduction:

The lesson today is about Daniel. His name has one of several meanings: "God is judge," "God has judged", "God is my Judge," or "God is my Defender." Daniel was an exilic prophet, along with Ezekiel. There were three deportations of Hebrews from Israel. He was in the first one. At the time of the lesson Daniel is about 15 years of age. He has three friends who are also teenagers: Hananiah, whose name was changed to Sudur-aku. According to Delitzsch, this name is Shadrach, the moon god, or illumined by the sun god; the name Mishael was changed to Meshach (Mishaku Meshach; "who is like Aku"); Azariah's name was changed to Abednego ("worshiper of Nego"). Daniel's name was changed to Belteshazzar. According to Dr. Pinches this name means "protect thou his life, O Bel". It was the Prince of the eunuchs who made the changes.

Translation, transliteration, interpretation;

v.	English	Hebrew	Pronunciation	Alternative meanings
8	purposed	שׂוּם	SŪM	to set, place, or resolve
	defile	גָּאַל	gā-AL	common, polluted, profane, unclean
	eunuch	סָרִיס	sā-RĪS	officer

It has been surmised that Daniel's reason for refusing was due to the condition of the meat, Lev. 3:17, 7:26, 17:10-14, 19:26, or its having been offered to idols.

v.	English	Hebrew	Pronunciation	Alternative meanings
9	favour	מַרְאֶה	mar-EH	appearance, good of countenance
	tender	רָכַךְ	rā-KHAKH	soft, weak, gentle, compassion
10	worse	זָעֵף	zā-AF	gloomy, sad, sadder
	sort	גִּיל	GĪL	circuit, circle, of your age
	endanger	חוֹב	KHŪV	make liable, be under penalty
12	pulse	זֵרְעִים	zē-rō-ĪM	seed, vegetable food
	prove	הסנ	nā-SĀH	try, put to test
13	countenance	מַרְאֶה	mar-EH	sight, aspect, view, form, appearance
15	fairer	טוֹב	TŌV	good in a very extensive sense, goodness
		טָהוֹר	tā-HŌR	pure, clean, clear
	skill	בִּין	BĪN	to discern, perceive

learning	לֶקַח	LE-qakh	instruction, doctrine, art of reading and writing
wisdom	חָכַם	khā-KHAM	understanding
dreams	חָלַם	khā-LAM	to speak

There are three important symbolic numbers in the lesson:
- Four men (#4 is a symbol of the world). The conviction of these four was being compared to the wordly.
- Three years duration by the King (#3 is the first word of completion); this was a type of the coming completion of the trials of the saints.
- 10 days (the #10 is symbolic of testimony, law, and responsibility, Ex. 12:3).
- Strong drink is a symbol of weakness rather than strength (10, Dan. 5:1; Prov. 20:1).
- Followers of God should have a made-up mind (8).
- Following the world will defile (8).
- Most teenagers are easily influenced (8).
- The Prince of the eunuch feared the King, but Daniel feared the King of Kings (10).
- Man looks on the outside, but God looks on the heart (10) 1 Sam. 16:7.
- God makes friends out of enemies, and sometimes footstools (9) Ps. 110:1; Heb. 10:13.
- God's people must be willing to be tried and proven (12).
- Man may change your name but only God can change your heart (7).
- All things work together for good to those who love the Lord (12-15) Rom. 8:28.
- The world should be able to tell the difference in God's people (13).
- God's people have meat that the world knows not of (Jn. 4:32).
- Every good and perfect gift comes from the Lord (17) Jas. 1:17.
- There are none like God's people (19) 1 Peter 2:9.
- Thru the Holy Spirit, we are become 10 times better than the world (20).

Amos Challenges Justice

AMOS 5:10-15, 21-24

Introduction:

Amos was the prophet to the Northern Kingdom (of Israel). Jeroboam was the King who was to reign over Israel for some 41 years (2 Ki. 14:23, 24). This was a period of prosperity in Israel; God had blessed them, but not because of their righteousness. This was an evil period which would lead to the fall of the Northern Kingdom (2 Ki. 17:5, 6).

Amos had had an applicable vision of fruit that was ripe for consuming. This was symbolic of Israel which was ripe for captivity because of their sins (Amos 8:2, 3, 6:4-6).

Amaziah, the wicked prophet had challenged Amos (Amos 7:10-13).

The Lord thru Amos had predicted that Israel's enemy (Assyria) would carry them away with fish hooks, and that Israel would continue to invite a life of sin (Amos 4:4).

Amos tells Israel to "prepare to meet thy God" (Amos 4:12).

Translation, transliteration, interpretation:

The name Amos עָמוֹס is believed to be a derivative of amuz, עָמוּז which means 'heavy of speech,' a bodily defect (Num. 12:6-8). The name Amos is translated from the Hebrew meaning "burden bearer".

The city of Tekoa was in the land of Judah, where Amos resided as a dresser of sycamore trees.

v.	English	Hebrew	Pronunciation	Alternative meanings
1	A lamentation is a period of sorrow and anguish.			
2	'Virgin of Israel', this is metaphoric language describing the character of Israel in the past.			
3	This verse is a prophecy of desolation against Israel.			
4	Here is God's continual promise of mercy.			
5	This verse gives a warning against Israel's sins in Bethel and Gilgal (Amos 4:4).			
10	rebuketh	וְכַח	vā-KHAKH	to set right, strong admonition, show to be wrong

In the gate: this was the place where the city fathers and leaders would assemble.

	abhor	תָּעַב	tā-AV	to detest, hate with indignation (Prov. 6:16-19)
11	trample	רָמַס	rā-MAS	to tread upon (Ps. 91:13; Isaiah 63:3)
	the exactions	הַשָּׁנ	nā-SHAH	to receive usury
	(alternatively)	נָגַשׂ	nā-GAS	to press a debt

Punishment for illegitimate wealth (Deut. 28:30).

12	ransom	גָּאַל	gā-AL	to redeem
	bribe	פָּדָה	pā-DĀH	(1 Sam. 12:3)

In the gate, where the poor have no influence, or can get no justice.

13	prudent	שָׂכַל	sā-KHAL	to behave wisely

An evil time, when men who speak the truth are imperiled. (Micah 2:3)

14 God's impending judgement will not be averted; although Amos continues to call to repent.

15	remnant	יָתַר	yā-TAR	the remainder, residue, the rest

21 God despised what was passing off for religion in Israel. The sacrifices were alright but the law of morality was being left out.

22	regard	נָבַט	nā-VAT	have respect to, taste, respect, consider
23	noise	הָמְה	hā-MĀH	the howling of a dog, or a bear, of the musical instruments
24	justice	צָדַק	tsā-DAQ	righteousness
	run down	גָּלַל	gā-LAL	well up, exceeding, mightily

Application:
- Wrong doers hate to be rebuked (10).
- The hope of the wicked is futile (11, Job 27:8; Prov. 11:7).
- God is aware of man's sins because He knoweth the heart where sin begins (12).
- A wise man knoweth when to keep his mouth shut (13).
- Good is a treasure which must be sought; evil can be found on every corner (14).
- What does God think of our solemn assemblies (21)?
- If songs of worship do not emanate from a righteous heart they are only noise.
- God cannot be bribed (21-23).
- Righteousness and justice should be plentiful (24).
- Sin cannot escape God's vision, nor judgement (1:3, 6, 9, 11, 13;, 2:1, 4, 6).
- Prosperity is not proof of Divine favour (5:3).
- Amos challenged justice, and justice is being challenged today!!!!!
- Obligation complements privilege (8:5).
- Without justice, religion is an empty sham (5:24).

Emmanuel's Birth

MATT. 1:18-25

Introduction:

The term, Emmanuel is Hebrew language for "God with us"; this phrase was from Isaiah's prophecy from God to King Ahaz. God is with us in Holy Spirit of Christ. The name Jesus (Joshua), is a contraction of Jehoshuah (Num. 13:16; 1 Chr. 7:27), meaning "Jehovah's helper," "help of Jehovah," "Jehovah is salvation," "Saviour"; "He will save His people from their sins" (as prophet, priest, King). Today's lesson is about His arrival.

Translation, transliteration, interpretation:

v.	English	Greek	Transliterated	Alternative meanings
18	birth	γένεσις	genesis (ginōmai)	to be born
	on this wise	οὕτως	houtōs	thus, in this way, under such circumstances
	espoused	μνηστευθείσης	mnēsteutheisēs	to ask in marriage, betrothel, affiance
	came together	συνελθεῖν	sunelthein	cohabitate, come together
	she was found	εὑρέθη	heurethē (heuriskō)	to find, to meet, to discover, to find out

A woman who was pledged to a man, if found impregnated by another man, they both were to be stoned (Deut. 22:23, 24).

| 19 | privily | λάθρα | lathra (lanthanō) | escape knowledge of observation, conceal, secretly |
| | not willing | ἐβουλήθη | eboulēthē | purpose, intend, desire |

Here Joseph was having a tragic struggle between his legal conscience and his love. Joseph was considering giving her a bill of divorcement (ἀπολῦσαι), apolusai, a release, from burden, a discharge, a dismissal with a fine (Deut. 24:1).

| 20 | He thought | ἐνθυμηθέντος | enthumēthentos | to ponder |
| | fear | φονηθῆς | phonēthes (phobeō) | terror, affright |

to take	παραλαβεῖν	paralabein,	take to one's side, receive to one's self
21 she shall bring forth	τέξεται	texetai (tiktō)	bear, bring forth children
22 Emmanuel (see above)			
24 bidden	προσέταξεν	prosetaxen	to order
25 knew her not	ἐγίνωσκεν	eginōsken (ginoskō)	carnal knowledge, ascertain by exam

Lessons from the lesson:

- Mary is not God's mother (1:25).
- Jesus arrived when God got ready (Gal. 4:4).
- The sin that Jesus was to save mankind of was "missing God's mark."
- Jesus' birth fulfilled prophecy (22, 23).
- God is still with us (1 Jn. 4:4).
- Unto us a child is born (Jesus); unto us a son is given (Christ) (Isaiah 9:6).
- Theological perspective:
- Virgin birth.
- The angel of the Lord.
- Perpetual virginity (Mary did not remain a virgin Matt. 13:55, 56; Mk. 6:3).
- Messiah (God's anointed).
- Pre-existence of Christ.
- Pre-incarnation of Christ.
- Of the Holy Ghost (genitive absolute).
- Christocentricity of Christ.
- Monotheistic (Kingdom).
- Dispensation of grace (Jn. 1:17).
- Prote-evangelium (the first gospel) Gen. 3:15.
- Jesus' first coming was in His humility (as a lamb).
- Jesus' second coming will be in His exaltation (as a lion).

Confirming Messiah's Birth

MATT. 2:7-10, 16-23

Introduction:

The birth of Jesus Christ is the fact of life. Men may doubt who He is or what He has done, but they cannot deny His arrival. The lesson today is a confirmation.

Translation, transliteration, interpretation:

Arnold Fruchtenbaum says that the star that the men from the east saw may not have been a real star, but the shekinah glory of God which: was low, bright, attracting attention, moving, hovering, moving east to west then north to south, directing, disappearing & reappearing.

v.	English	Greek	Transliterated	Alternative meanings
2:3	troubled	ἐταράχθη	etarachthē	agitated, aggravated
2:4	demanded	ἐπυνθάνετο	epunthaneto	inquire, ascertain
2:5	The scribes quoted from the prophet Micah 5:2.			
2:7	privily	λάνθρα	lanthra	secretly, unnoticed, to escape knowledge of
	diligently	ἠκρίβωσεν	ēkribōsen	exactly, accurately
	time	χρόνον	chronon	age of star's appearance, duration, point of lapse
	appearing	φαινομένου	phainomenou	be seen, bring to light
2:8	enquired		exetasate	search out
	young child	παιδίου	paidiou (pais)	a child, youth
	worship	προσκυνήσω	proskunēskō	do homage
2:9		ἰδού	idou	to call attention to
	They saw the same star; this time it wasn't moving to reveal the city which they now knew, but the place.			
2:10	they rejoiced exceedingly	σφόδρα	sphodra	much, greatly, intense
2:13	Joseph is warned in a dream to evacuate to Egypt.			

2:16	mocked	ἐνεπαίχθη	enepaichthē	deride, treat with scorn
			(empaizō)	
2:17	fulfilled	ἐπληρώθη	eplērōthē	completed

2:18   Rama: this was a city, 5 miles north of Jerusalem (see Jeremiah 40:1; Gen. 35:19). Rachel is the symbolic mother of the nation Israel (she had been the wife of Jacob). She symbolically was lamenting because the kingdom of Judah was being captured by the Chaldeans

2:19   Joseph is directed in another dream to return to Israel (see Hosea 11:1). Notice from Matt. 2:11, Jesus is in a house, also He is a young child.

Lessons from the lesson:

- God's people should know His word (2:5).
- The wise men from the east obviously knew from prophecy or revelation that a King was born.
- Sometimes non-Christians know more of the Scriptures than Christians do (2:2).
- Searching the Scriptures should be a public venture (4, 5).
- Men often make pretence of piety (8).
- Some men are brutally jealous of their position (8).
- God often gives directions thru signs in nature (9).
- Evil people have evil minds (8).
- It is interesting that God had spoken to Joseph 3 times in dreams.
- Men are wise who follow God's directions (12).
- Evil people see Christ and Christians as rivals (7, 16).
- People who do not know Jesus, often have to ask from others who are supposed to know but don't.
- When nothing else stops wicked men, death always does it (20).

Strengthened in Temptation

MATT. 4:1-11

Introduction:

The writer to the Hebrews (2:18) relates that Christ suffered being tempted, and consequently is able to succour them that are tempted.

(4:15) "For we have not a high priest which can not be touched with the feeling of our infirmities, but was in all points tempted like as we are, yet without sin."

The apostle to the Corinthians wrote (10:13) "there hath no temptation taken you but such as is common to man; but God is faithful, who will not suffer you to be tempted above that ye are able; but will with the temptation also make a way to escape, that ye may be able to bear it."

Today our lesson, as you can see, is about temptation; Jesus setting an example for us.

(Jas. 1:14) "But every man is tempted, when he is drawn away of his own lust and enticed."

Jesus was driven up of the Holy Spirit to be tempted of the devil.

Translation, transliteration, interpretation:

v.	English	Greek	Transliterated	Alternative meanings
1	tempted	πειρασθῆσαι	peirasthēsia (peirazō)	to test, to try, solicit to sin (negatively)
	was led up	ἀνήχθη	anēchthē (anagō)	to conduct, to lead, to lead out
2	having fasted	νηστεύσας	nēstausas	to eat little or nothing for a period of time

The number 40 is significant; a period of testing. Moses fasted for 40 days (Ex. 34:28).

	hungered	ἐπείνασεν	epeinasen	
3	tempter	πειράζων	peirozōn	the slanderer (diabolou)
	if	εἰ	ei	can also be translated 'since'

Exercise your power as son, prove to yourself.

	the tempter came to Him	προσελθὼν	proselthōn	to go to
	command	εἰπὲ	eipe	to speak to
4	it is written	γέγραπται	gegraptai	it stands written, and is still in force, Deut. 8:3
	every word	παντὶ ῥήματι	panti rhēmati	(pan = all, rhema = word)
	proceedeth	ἐκπορευομένῳ	ekporeuomenō	going out, departing from
	mouth	στόματος	stomatos	
6	cast thyself down	βάλε σεαυτὸν κάτω	bale seauton katō	ballō = throw + seauton = thyself
	charge	ἐντελεῖται	enteleitai (telos)	result, ultimate destiny

(Ps. 91:11 The tempter leaves out "in all thy ways" from the verse).

6	bear	ἀροῦσίν	arousin (airō)	
	dash	προσκόψῃς	proskopsēs (proskoptō)	to stumble

Do not tempt the Lord thy God (Deut. 6:16).

8	exceeding	λίαν	lian	much, great
	kingdoms	βασιλείας	basileias	realm governed by a King
	sheweth	δείκνυσιν	deiknusin	to point out, to exhibit
9	I will give	δώσω	dōsō (didōmi)	to give, bestow, supply, to distribute
10	(Him) only	μόνῳ	monō	sole, lone, without accompaniment (Deut. 6:13)
11	ministered	διηκόνουν	diekonoun (diakoneō)	attendant, servant, (maybe with food) as Elijah (1 Ki. 19:6)
	leaveth	ἀφίησιν	aphiēsin	

For a season (Lk. 4:13): until a good opportunity.

Lessons from the lesson:

- The same Spirit who anointed Jesus at the baptism, led Him to be tempted of the devil (4:1).
- Being tempted is not a sin; it's how one handles temptation that matters (4:1).
- It is a dangerous thing to take temptation too lightly (4:1).
- If Jesus, God's Son, was tested, how much more will we be tested (4:1)?
- The devil's temptation came after 40 days of deprivation; at our weakest moments (4:2).
- Miracles do not always verify who Jesus is (Jn. 6:26).

- Sinful men live by bread alone (4:4).
- Jesus didn't need stones to make bread, He made all things (Jn. 1:3).
- The children of God live on His word (Acts 17:28).
- Our prayer to God should be "lead us not" & "leave us not" into temptation (Matt. 6:13).
- If a need is not satisfied properly by the needy, it is improper (4:5).
- Satan and the ungodly may quote Scripture but they do not follow them. They impress hearers; they are used for their own benefit (4:6).
- The Lord tests, tries, and proves us, but we are not to tempt Him (4:6, 7).
- We have the power to resist Satan (Jas. 4:7).
- Spiritual victories are not always visible (4:11).
- Jesus reigns by way of the Cross; not by escaping from it (2 Tim. 2:12).
- God's law demands worship and service (Deut. 6.13, 10:20, Matt. 4:10, 11).
- If Satan gets men to fall down and worship him, they will serve him (4:9).
- What does Satan have to offer (1 Jn. 2:16: pride of life, lust of flesh, lust of eyes, 4:9)?
- Satan may leave but he's coming back until he is stopped permanently.
- Satan's temptation to Jesus is being made to us: satisfy yourself, prove yourself, profit yourself (1 Jn. 2:16).
- Satan's 3rd offer to Jesus was legitimate: he is the God of this world (1 Cor. 4:4) and prince of power of the air (Eph. 2:2).

Miracles of Compassion

MATTHEW 9:18-31, 35-38

Introduction:

Miracles are attestations of Divine revelation by means of Divine power. The purpose of miracles is to verify, confirm, authenticate or give credence to the Revelation of God to the world. In spite of the many miracles in the world that God continues to work, there are those who continue to reject Him and deny His existence. In our lesson today, we will see three clear examples of God's highest revelation: that are in Jesus the Christ, our Lord.

In our subject, the word miracle is the Greek word, σημειον (*sēmeion*) sign.

Also, the word compassion is the Greek word, ἐλεέω (*eleeō*) the affections of the heart, tender affections, chief intestines, entrails, bowels.

Translation, interpretation, transliteration:

v.	English	Greek	Transliterated	Alternative meanings
18	daughter	θυγάτηρ	thugatēr	
	ruler	ἄρχων	archōn	magistrate, authority, principality
	worshipped	προσεκύνει	prosekunei	reverence, give homage
	dead	ἐτελεύτησεν	eteleutēsen	has died, closing, finality, ultimate destiny
20	issue	αἱμορροοῦσα	haimorroousa	a flux or effusion of blood
	behind	ὄπισθεν	opisthen	at the back. after, things which are behind
	hem	κρασπέδου	kraspedou	border, fringe, tassel (Num. 15:38)
21	whole	σωθήσομαι (σώζω)	sōthēsomai (sōzō)	rescue, save, preserve, heal, deliver
	within herself	καταρτίζω	katarizō	restore to health reflexive pronoun (3rd person, one's self)

68

22	having turned about	ἐπιστραφαὶς	epistraphais	turn towards, about, around
	good comfort	θάρσει	tharseō	courage, confident, bold
	faith	πίστις	pistis	be induced, convinced, to the favour of
	made thee whole	σέσωκέν (σώζω)	sesōken	hath cured thee
23	minstrels	αὐλητὰς	aulētas	flute players
	making a noise	θορυβούμενον	thoruboumenon	Tumult, commotion, disturbance

There were various motives for their presence: sympathy, food, money etc (Jer. 9:17).

24	give place	ἀναχωρεῖτε	anachōreite	withdraw, go away, depart
	sleepeth	καθεύδει	katheudei	the sleep of death
	laughed	κατεγέλων	katelegōn	deride, jeer, scorn
25	put forth	ἐξεβλήθη	exeblēthē	put out, expel, eject by force, cast out
	maid	κοράσιον	korasion	damsel
26	fame	φήμη	phēmē	report, tell forth
27	thence	ἐκεῖθεν	ekeithen	there, thither
	blind	τυφλοὶ	tuphloi	
	crying	κράζοντες	krazontes	cry for help, earnest supplication, sorrow, wail
	mercy	ἐλέησον	eleēson	pity, compassion
28	able	δύναμαι	dunamai	power, strength, ability
29	eyes	ὀφθαλμῶν	ophthalmōn	to see, behold, look
30	were opened	ἠνεώχθησαν	ēneōchthēsan	to be opened, act of opening

Demonstrated in Acts of Healing

MATT. 9:27-34; 11:2-6

Introduction:

In this quarter we are examining evidences of Jesus as Messiah; today's lesson relates the works of Jesus to show that He did what only the Messiah could do. His miracles were for the purpose of authenticating His claims. Jesus came primarily for spiritual healing, not physical healing.

Jesus is presumed to be in Capernaum (9:1).

Translation, transliteration, interpretation:

v.	English	Greek	Transliterated	Alternative meanings
9:27	Here, two blind men are following Jesus, addressing Him as descendant of David, whose kingdom is to be everlasting. Later, other blind men would call on Him for healing (20:30).			
	mercy	ἐλέησον	eleēson (eleeō, eleos)	compassion, kindness, pity
9:28	Jesus only acknowledged them after entering the house (perhaps the house of Peter). Jesus waited until entering the house, perhaps He didn't want to attract much attention.			
	believe ye	πιστεύετε	pisteuete (pisteuō, peltho)	persuade, convince, influence
	able	δύναμαι	dunamai	power, energy, strength
9:29	touched	ἥψατο	hepsato (haptō)	to contact physically,
	Jesus did not need to touch them to heal them. This was probably a touch of sympathy.			
	according to	κατὰ	kata	as is, as much as
	Obviously, the men had faith in Him because they were healed.			
9:30	straightly charged	ἐνεβριμήθη	enebrimēthē	of snorting horses, (men with anger)
	see	ὁρᾶτε	horate	
	no one	μηδεὶς	medeis	

	let know	γινωσκέτω	ginōsketō	
9:31	fame	διεφήμισαν	diephēmisan (diaphemizō)	make known
9:32	dumb	κωφὸν	kōphon	blunt, dull of hearing
	possessed	δαιμονιζόμενον	daimonizomenon	inhabited by power of a demon
9:33	marvelled	ἐθαύμασαν	ethaumasan (thaumazo, thambos)	wonder, amaze
9:34	prince of devils	ἄρχοντι	archonti (archōn, archē)	evil headship, authority

11:2 John the Baptist is confined in prison at Macarus, east of the Dead Sea. John was depressed. He had already accepted the Holy Spirit's identification of Jesus at His baptism. Here he asks the same question that others had asked of Him (Jn. 1:21), "are you the one?"

11:3	should come	ἐρχόμενος	erchomenos	the coming one
	look for it	προσδοκῶμεν	prosdokōmen	be expectant
	another	ἕτερον	heteron	someone else

11:12 The impatient followers of Christ were trying to take it by force.

11:4 Jesus was busy when John's disciples came, so they were eye witnesses of His credentials.

4:12 Jesus had departed to Galilee when He heared that John was in prison. John needed encouragement, reassurance for him. Jesus wasn't baptizing with the Holy Spirit and with fire; He is not setting up His kingdom, and He is not getting him out of prison. John's disciples had seen Isaiah 35:5, 6 being fulfilled by Jesus and had such a msg. to give him.

11:6	offended	σκανδαλισθῇ	skandalisthē	occasion of stumbling, impediment

- Often our healing is according to our faith (9:29, Jas. 1:6, 7).
- Jesus' miracles were not intended to over shadow His misson but authenticate Him (30).
- We should not take demons too lightly (32).
- God's goodness is called evil by evil men (34).
- The joy of God's salvation and healing cannot be restrained (31).
- The prince of demons will not cast himself out (34, Matt. 12:25-30).

- Often in distress, many faithful are tempted to doubt (11:2, 3).
- Remembering God's love and deliverance and purpose can restore our faith (4, 5).
- Actions do speak louder than words (5, 6).
- There are times when it seems that God is not working fast enough for us (Matt. 11:3-6).

Declared in Prayer

MATT. 11:25-30

Introduction:

Jesus has been denouncing the major cities in which He had shown His works. In each of them the inhabitants had rejected Him thru unbelief. Chorazin, Bethsaida, Tyre, Sidon, Capernaum, and Sodom, each had rejected revealed truth. In our lesson today, Jesus is praying to the Father with thanksgiving for His revelation. He is also extending an invitation of salvation to all who had been yoked up to the teaching of the Pharisees, which had made them weary and burdened.

Translation, transliteration, interpretation:

v.	English	Greek	Transliterated	Alternative meanings
25	I thank thee	ἐξομολογοῦμαί	exomologoumai	to declare, profess, accord, praise openly

Here Jesus is not just thanking God, but worshipping and praising Him in prayer.

	English	Greek	Transliterated	Alternative meanings
	hid	ἐκρυψας	ekrupsas (apokruptō)	to hide away, withhold from sight or knowledge

See also the parallel passage Lk. 10:21-24. Much of God's revelation in Jesus had been hidden in parables, to conceal from the egoists. See Matt. 13:10, 11.

	English	Greek	Transliterated	Alternative meanings
	wise	σοφῶν	sophōn	shrewd, sagacious, clever, learned
	prudent	συνετῶν	sunetōn	to perceive, understand, discern, intellect

This was sarcasm, regarding those who thought themselves wise, but were not, regarding Jesus.

	English	Greek	Transliterated	Alternative meanings
	babes	νηπίοις	nēpiois	infant, below manhood, simple, unlearned
	revealed	ἀπεκάλυψας	apekalupsas	disclose, manifest, appear, declare
26	seemed	εὐδοκία	eudokia	delight, think well, approve, favour

| 27 | knoweth | ἐπιγνώσκει | epignōskei | observation, to arrive at knowledge, see John 1:18 |
| | | | | |

Christ is God's revelation (Jn. 14:9).

28	labour	κοπιῶντες	kopiōntes (kopiaō, kopto)	bewail, beat self in mourning, uneasy
	laden	πεφορτισμένοι	pephortismenoi	state of weariness, burdened
	rest	ἀναπαύσω	anapausō (anapauō)	sooth, rejuvenation, refresh, rest up
30	yoke	ζυγός	zugos	obligation, service
	learn	μάθετε	mathete (manthanō)	be taught, experience, practice, acquire, inquiry
	easy	χρηστὸς	chrēstos (chraomai)	kindly, good and useful, behave towards

Lessons from the lesson:

- There is a difference between those who think they know and those who realize they don't (25).
- God is not impressed with human wisdom (25).
- Anyone who claims God but rejects Jesus is deceiving himself (27).
- To know Christ is to find relief (28).
- Christ's yoke is pleasing, satisfying, acceptable (30).
- There are degrees of punishment for those who reject Jesus (Rom. 1:18, 19, 20; Matt. 11:21-23).

Revealed in Rejection

MATT. 13:54-58

Introduction:

It is amazing how many people claim to know God, the Father, but refuse to accept His revelation in Jesus (Jn. 14:9). In the lesson today, Jesus is making His second trip to Nazareth during His public ministry. Nazareth of course is in Galilee; this is where Jesus spent His boyhood. His first teaching tour of Nazareth is recorded in Luke 4:16-30. Today's text is also recorded by Mark 6:1-6. In today's passage Jesus has just concluded teaching in parables about the Kingdom of heaven. He had spoken in parables both to conceal and to reveal (Matt. 13:10, 11). See Matt. 11:25; 2 Cor. 4:3, 4.

After this, He decides to return to Nazareth for the second time. The people of the town are confused; wondering how He could have such knowledge without having any formal training; and how could He be the fulfillment of Isaiah's prophecy (Isaiah 61:1, 2).

Translation, transliteration, interpretation:

v.	English	Greek	Transliterated	Alternative meanings
54	His own country	πατρίδα αὐτοῦ	patrida autou	origination
	Mk. 6:1	ἐξῆλθεν	exēlthen	
	Jesus came out			

Jesus had spent some time in Capernaum; this out going is perhaps in reference thereto.

	astonished	ἐκπλήσσεσθαι	ekplēssesthai	struck out of one's senses or wits, astound, amaze
	whence	πόθεν	pothen	origin, source, in what way
	wisdom	σοφία	sophia	
55	carpenter	τέκτονος	tektonos	one who works in wood

Matthew calls Jesus the carpenter's son; in the Mark passage He is called the carpenter (6:3). Nazareth may not have had but one carpenter during that time; (Joseph and Jesus). Mary did have other children after the birth of Jesus; at least 4 boys and 2 girls. Also, Jesus was fully man and fully God.

57	offended	ἐσκανδαλίζοντο	eskandalizonto	to stumble at, be repelled by, to turn against
	honor	ἄτιμος	atimos	credit, esteem, glory
58	unbelief	ἀπιστίαν	apistian (apisteuō)	disbelief, false, faithless, violate faith

Even Nathanial in reference to Nazareth wondered (Jn. 1:46).

Lessons from the lesson:
- Nazareth was a microcosm of the whole nation (in unbelief and rebellion, Mk. 5:58).
- Spiritual truth is offensive to persons who are determined to continue a worldly lifestyle (Lk. 4:28, 29).
- Many become violent when confronted the truth of the gospel (Lk. 4:28, 29).
- The gospel convicts and arouses guilt in the guilty (Matt. 13:57).
- There are many who do not want their worldly life style interrupted (57).
- Often those who know us best are hardest to convince of our spiritual gifts (Matt. 13:55).
- Many persons base their expectations on vague knowledge of the past (Matt. 13:55).
- The disbelief of many often blocks the will and purpose of God (Mk. 5:5; Matt. 13:58).
- No venue is too small or lowly for preaching God's Word (Mk. 6:5).
- The truth of the gospel is hidden from many unbelievers (2 Cor. 4:3, 4).
- The same gospel that saves often condemns (Matt. 25:41-46).
- Often when a familiar one comes into prominence, jealousy is envoked (Lk. 4:22, 28, 29).
- Jesus was never surprised by evil responses; neither should we be (Matt. 13:57, 58).
- Many people are offended very easily, and for the wrong reason (Matt. 13:57).
- Those who reject our Lord will be rejected by our Lord (1 Pe. 2:7, 8; Matt. 7:13).

Christ as Messiah

MATT. 16:13-23

Introduction:

Only 4 times is the word Messiah literally written in the Scriptures; twice in the prophecy of Daniel (9:25, 26) and twice in the gospel recorded by John (1:41, 4:25).

The word is the Aramaic χριστος, christos (chrio), meaning to anoint, or anointed one. It is derived from the Hebrew מָשַׁח mā-SHAKH, meaning anoint. The fact is that Jesus Christ is the anointed Son of God; anointed meaning authorized, appointed, empowered.

Translation, transliteration, interpretation:

v.	English	Greek	Transliterated	Alternative meanings

13 Caesarea Philippi: there were 2 locations called Caesarea; 1 on the coast of Samaria, and another located in upper Galilee. These were named after Caesar who was Roman Emperor, this one in our lesson was also named after Phillip, ruler of upper Galilee.

14 The people had varying opinions of who Jesus was. Some thought that He was: John the Baptist, having returned from the dead (From Herod's execution); Elijah, who had been predicted to return (Mal. 4:5, 6; Jn. 1:21; Matt. 17:11, 12, 27:47); Jeremiah or another prophet (Matt. 16:14).

16 Son of God, (not inferior to but indentified with)

   living   ζῶντος   zōntos (zaō)   life

   Peter had made this confession before (John 6:69.

18 this rock   πέτρα   petra   stone, Aramaic כֵּיפָא (KĒ-fā)

   When Jesus first met Simon, He told Him that He would be called *Cephas* (*Petros*); כֵּיף (KĒF). 'Upon *this rock* I will build my Church.' What was Jesus referring to build the Church on? Was it on Peter (according to Chrysostom, Olashausen, De witte, and others)?

Was it on Peter's testimony (according to Calvin, Koppe, Harless, Meyer, Eadre, Ellicott)? According to Milton Terry there is room for 3 points of view:

1. Genitive of apposition (the apostles and prophets are the foundation Eph. 2:20-22, Gal. 2:9 Rev. 21:9)
2. Gentive of originating cause (the foundation was laid by the apostles and prophets, 1 Cor. 3:10, Rom. 15:20).
3. Genitive of possession (the apostles, prophets, and all believers are in the foundation, Jesus Christ being the chierf corner stone, 1 Peter 2:4, 5, according to Beza, Bucer, Alford).

There is no Church without Christ Jesus.

The Church is the pillar and ground of truth.

Petros of Matt. 16:18 has become a living stone (*lithos*) and representative of the believers (see 1 John 4:15; Rom. 10:9).

Jesus in going from *petros* masculine gender to *petras* feminine gender indicates that the Church is not built on Peter the man, but the confessor, type, and representative of the people

19	keys	κλεῖδας	skleidas	
	bind	δήσῃς	dēsēs	(by unbelief) fall short, hinder, confine, prohibit, bundle as tare
	loose	λύσῃς	lusēs	hope, redeem, relieve, unfasten, liberate, dismiss, ransom

All of this is with the sanction of God, the Father.

Here are four definite articles: the anointed, the Christ, the Son, the God who lives.

22	rebuke	ἐπιτιμᾶν	epitimav	allege as a crimination, chide, reprimand, censure
	taken	προσλαβόμενος	proslabamenos	take or draw to one's self
23	savourest	φρονεῖς	phroneis (phren)	think, mind, opinion, take thought

Lessons from the text:
- God is alive (16).
- Flesh and blood cannot reveal godly things (17).
- Hell has gates; heaven has doors and windows. The Church will storm hell's gates to set the captives free (18).
- Heaven confirms the actions of Spirit filled men (19).
- Knowing who Jesus is, is not the same as knowing Him (14).
- There are untold blessings in knowing Jesus (16).

- Satan within Peter desires to transform him from a petra (lively stone) to a stumbling stone (23).
- If men are focusing Jesus' death on the here and now, then, it doesn't make much sense (22).

Repentance Leads to Community

MK. 1:1-8; MATT. 3:1-3

Introduction:

The land of Israel was divided into three sections: Galilee, Samaria, and Judea. John was preaching and baptizing in the Southern part of Israel. The river Jordan ran north and south thru the land. The Israelites were used to baptism, being that the proselytes were baptized into Judaism.

Translation, transliteration, interpretation:

v.	English	Greek	Transliterated	
Matt. 3				
1	wilderness	ἠρέμαις	hēremais	deserted place, not in the city
2	repent	μεταωοεῖτε	metanōeite	to turn the mind around,שׁוּב, SHŪV turn back Ezekiel 14:6, 18:30
	kingdom	βασιλεία	basileia	the reign of a King
	at hand	ἤγγικεν	ēggiken (ēggizō, ēggus)	to approach, close at hand, impending
3	spoken of	ῥηθεὶς	rhētheis (rheō)	to say, to 'speak of
	Here Matthew gives His narration of Isaiah 40:3.			
	voice	φωνὴ	phōnē	speech, discourse, outcry
	one crying	βοῶντος	boōntos (boaō, boe)	exclamation, proclaim, cry out
	prepare	ἑτοιμάσατε	etoimasate (etoimazō)	make ready, get ready
4	way	ὁδὸν	hodon	approach, means of access, direction, system
	paths	τρίβους	tribous	a beaten track, worn track
	straight	εὐθείας	eutheias (euthus)	upright, true
	Elijah seems to have been John's role model (2 Ki. 1:8).			
Mark 1				

1	gospel	εὐαγγελίου	euaggeliou (euaggelizō)	glad tidings
	it is written	γέγραπται	gegraptai	it has been written

See Mal. 3:1, Isaiah 40:3, Lk. 7:27 (this is He, Elijah is come).

	I send	ἀποστέλλω	apostellō	
	messenger	ἄγγελόν	aggelon (aggelonazō)	one sent to tell, angel
	shall prepare	κατασκευάσει	kataskeuasei	put in readiness
4	baptism of repentance	βάπτισμα	baptisma metanoias	baptism marked by repentance
	remission	ἄφεσιν	aphesin (aphiemi)	send away, dismiss, leave, depart
5	confessing	ἐξομολογούμενοι	exomologoumenoi	to agree, bend over one's self, make avowal
6	hair	τρίχας	trichas	

This was not the skin of the camel but the hair woven thru the rough material

	girdle	ζώμην	zemen	(as a belt)
	leather	δερματίνην	dermatinēn (derō)	skin of an animal
	locusts	ἀκρίδας	akridas (akris)	this is said to have been the insect, which many considered palatable
	honey	μέλι	meli	made by bees, particularly in the rocks and mountains
7	mightier	ἰσχυρότερός	ischuroteros	depreciation
	worthy	ἱκανὸς	hikanos	befitting, fit
	latchet	ἱμάντα	himanta	thong which held the shoes together
	stoop	κύψας	kupsas	bend forward, having stooped

Lessons from the lesson:
- God's Kingdom has come. We can see its signs and proof (Matt. 3:2).
- Great crowds came out to hear John. Many preachers begin with large crowds but turn them away (5).
- Many use the crowd for their own purpose (self aggrandizement, 5).
- Christ is God's King of His Kingdom (Matt. 3:2).

- Now is the time to cry out (Matt. 3:1, Joel 2:1).
- This beginning was not Christ's beginning but the gospel's (Mk. 1:1).
- That which was written aforehand was written for our admonition (1 Cor. 10:11), for doctrine, illustration, to refute false teaching, and to show fulfillment.
- God's way is a straight way (2).
- We must preach repentance and confession (4, Acts 19:1-5).
- The woman who touched Jesus' garment was not worthy either; but He accepted her (7, Mk. 5:28).
- John wasn't worthy but Jesus eulogized him (Lk. 7:28).

Looking for Jesus

MARK 1:35-45

Introduction:

The servants of the Lord Jesus are awaiting His arrival. The writer to the Hebrews affirmed that we look to Him who is the author and finisher of our faith. We do not look for Him, but to Him. He is not lost, we know where He is. He has a time and place for His arrival.

History:

- Mark's Roman name was Markus; his Hebrew name was John.
- He was nephew to Barnabus, and son of Mary, who was devout and courageous (Acts 12:12-17, Col. 4:1).
- He accompanied Paul and Barnabus on their missionary journey (departing from them at Perga).
- Mark was known as the disciple of Peter (1 Pe. 5:13).
- Mark and Paul were reconciled in Rome (Acts 13:13).
- Some believe that Mark was the unnamed man of Mk. 14:51.
- There are many prominent words in his writing: εὐθὺς, euthus, used some 40 times, translated: 'forth-with, immediately, straightway, anon'.
- Mark's writing of the gospel is said to have been written from Rome between A.D. 48-52, especially for Gentiles.
- Written before the fall of Jerusalem (ch. 13).
- Nero, the Emperor had burned Rome (A.D. 64), blaming Christians for it (to persecute them).

Mark uses many Aramaic words or phrases:

boanerges	sons of thunder (3:17)
talethacumi	damsel arise (5:14)
korban	gift, sacred treasury (7:1)
ephphatha	be opened (7:34)
abba	father (14:36)

Latin words and phrases:

centurio	(15:39)
quadrans	(12:42)
flagellare	*(15:15)*
speculator	*(6:27)*
census	(12:14)
sextarius	*(7:4)*
praetorium	*(15:6)*

Mark records Jesus foretelling His own death and resurrection, 8:31, 32.

Translation, transliteration, interpretation:

v.	English	Greek	Transliterated	Alternative meanings
35	in the morning	πρωῒ	prōi	
	last watch	ἔννυχα	ennucha	early watch 3-6 am
	solitary	ἔρημον	erēmon	desert, alone
36	followed after	κατεδίωχεν	katediōchen	hunted down, went after, hard on track, follow perseveringly
37	found	εὑρόντες	heurontes	find, detect, discover

"All men seek thee" a note of reproach, as "where have you been?" Peter is eager to see more of Jesus' work in his home town.

38 They were surprised that Jesus didn't stay there with the crowd (see Luke 4:43, Isaiah 9:12).

	next	ἐξομένας	exomenas	cling to, border upon, neighboring
39	cast out	ἐκβάλλων	ekballōn	eject by force, expel, extract
40	clean	καθαρίσαι	katharisai	cleanse, make pure (from leprosy)
41	being moved with compassion	σπλαγχνισθεὶς	splagchnistheis	intestines, bowels (heart)
42	immediately	εὐθὺς	euthus	(see above in history)
44	show thyself	δεῖξον	deixon	cause to be seen, demonstrate
	priest	ἱερεῖ	hierei	(Lev. 14:2-31)

Jesus respected God's law and showed the power of God at work.

44	Moses commanded (what Moses ordered)			
	offer for cleansing	προσέταξεν	prosetaxen	

for testimony	μαρτύριον	marturion	judicial witness, testifier
45 publish	κηρύσσειν	kērussein	

Lessons from the lesson:
- God's work often requires an early start; and, also refusal of bodies' need for sleep and food (35).
- God is on the "anytime line" (35).
- Prayer is not to be considered a chore but a voluntary desire (35).
- Prayer should be in a solitary place (secret closet) (35), free from distractions, people need not see us praying.
- It would be great if more people in the Church shared this zeal to pray (35).
- Prayer tunes us in to God's will and way (35).
- Often man's expectations are overturned by the purposes of God (38, 43, 44).
- The message of Christ is not for just a few but for all (38, Heb. 11:6).
- The leper's body language made his request more sincere. So will ours (40).
- Here would be a student inspecting the teacher's work (44).
- Many seek Christ for selfish reasons (37, Jn. 6:26).

Recognizing Jesus

MARK 5:1-13, 18-20

Introduction:

Satan's plan is to keep people from recognizing Jesus; in spite of all of Satan's attempts we see and recognize Jesus. From Scripture prophecy, from witnesses, from His blessings, from fulfillment of His promises and from numerous other ways. We shall recognize Him when He makes His appearance in the rapture and the resurrection. Hallelujah!!!!

The country of the gadarenes was referring to one of the 10 cities around A.D. 65, after the Roman conquest of Syria. There were 10 Greek cities. 9 of them were east of the Jordan River; Pella, Gadara, Hippos, Dion, Philadelphia, Gerasa, Canatha, Damascus, Raplana, and Scythopolis, which was west of the Jordan River. These cities were called Decapolis (ten cities).

Jesus had just calmed a storm out in the Sea of Galilee, and was about to calm another storm in the heart of a tormented man.

Translation, transliteration, interpretation:

v.	English	Greek	Transliterated	Alternative meanings
2	immediately	εὐθὺς	euthus	anon, straightway, forthwith (a word used over 40 times by Mark)
	met	ὑπήντησεν	hupēntēsen (apantaō)	to meet, encounter

It was almost as if Jesus had an appointment with this man.

	tombs	μνημείων	mnēmeiōn	memorial, monument, sepulchre
	unclean	ἀκαθάρτῳ	akathartō	not clean
3	dwelling	κατοίκησιν	katoikēsin	inhabit, abode, indwell
	bind	δῆσαι	dēsai (deō)	confine, impede, hinder
	chain	ἁλύσει	alusei	a chain
4	fetters	πέδαις	pedais, (pedas, pede, peza)	the foot

86

	broken	συντετρῖφθαι	suntetriphthai	break in pieces, crush, bruise, shatter, break power of
	tame	δαμάσαι	damasai	subdue
5	crying	κράζων	krazōn	wail, lament, a cry for help
	cutting	κατακόπων	katakoptōn	cut, dash in pieces
	stones	λίθοις	lithois	(lithos)
6	having seen	ἰδὼν	idōn (oraō)	look, mark, see, observe
	afar	μακρόθεν	makrothen (mēkos)	distance, remote, from far
	worship	προσεκύνησεν	prosekunēsen	adore, homage, reverence
7	adjure	ὁρκίζω	orkizō	by oath, a solemn promise
	torment	βασανίσῃς	basanisēs	test metals, test others by torture
	what have i to do with thee	τί ἐμοὶ καὶ σοί	ti emoi kai soi	what to me and to thee
8	come out	ἔξελθε	exelthe (exerchomai)	come out, go away, come forth
9	what is thy name	τί ὄνομά σοι	ti onoma soi	
	legion	λεγιὼν	legiōn	an indefinite great number
		A Roman legion was 6826 soldiers.		
	many	πολλοί	polloi	much, large, great
10	besought	παρεκάλει	parekalei	call for, invite, send for, beg, entreat, implore
		The demon's real home was the abyss.		
	country	χώρας	choras	province, tract, district, territory
13	gave them leave	ἐπέτρεψεν	epetrepsen	allowed
20	marvel	ἐθαύμαζον	ethaumazon	filled with wonder, astonished (see Isaiah 11:1)

- Jesus' ministry went beyond the Jews (1).
- It was almost as if Jesus had an appointment with this man (2).
- Demons feel at home among the tombs of the dead (3).
- Demons can put a man in misery (4, 5).
- Satan offers power, but at a terrible price (1-5).

- The demons had no mercy on others, yet they wanted mercy from Jesus. Jesus gave it (7, 10).
- Satan and demons are fearful of Jesus; why should we be fearful of them (6, 7).
- Spiritual warfare is not for the fearful (8).
- The demons realized that they must obey Jesus (7, 10).
- The demons spoke as one, united in evil (9).
- They planned to live in the pigs, not knowing that the pigs would act this way (13).
- After the pigs died, the demons probably got in another weak person (13).
- It is better for pigs to perish then men (13).
- The people had been afraid of the man, now they were afraid of Jesus (15).
- They found the man in his right mind, and he had put his clothes on (Lk. 8:27, 35).
- The man wanted to stay with Jesus (possibly fearing a return of the demons) (18).
- The man may have driven all his friends away (19).
- The man obeyed Jesus and did as we should be doing (20).

Pleading for Mercy

MARK 7:24-30

Introduction:

The definition of mercy is pity, fore-bearance, favour in distress, compassionate treatment. In the lesson today, Jesus has left Galilee traveling northward, arriving at the borders of Tyre and Sidon which are cities of Gentiles; taken in the Macedonian conquest. These cities were on the coast of the Mediterranean Sea and had been besieged by both Nebuchadnezzar and Alexander. Jesus did not do many works here (Matt. 11:21, 22; Luke 4:26). This area was about 20 miles westward from Capernaum.

In the Septuagint version, Canaan is the same as Phoenicia; where the races were mixed.

It was here that Jesus met a Phoenician woman who spoke the Syrian language. She was also Grecian. This same event can be found in Matthew 15:21-28.

Translation, transliteration, interpretation:

Jesus is trying to get some rest, in a secluded area. The house that He enters into is unknown.

Many years before, the King of Tyre had been very helpful to David and Solomon with material for the Temple (1 Ki. 5).

v.	English	Greek	Transliterated	Alternative meanings
24	not be hid	οὐκ ἠδυνήθη	ouk ēdunēthē	not able to be unnoticed or concealed
		λαθεῖν	lathein	
25	young daughter	θυγάτριον	thugatrion	having tender touch
	unclean	ἀκάθαρτον	akatharton	spiritually unclean
	having come	ἐλθοῦσα	elthousa (erchomai)	to come or go pass
	fell	προσέπεσεν	prosepesen	
	feet	πόδας	podas	
26	Greek	Ἑλληνίς	Hellēnis	
	Syrophenician, see introduction.			
	besough	ἠρώτα	ērōta	request, kept at it

89

| devil | δαιμόνιον | diamonion | demon |
| cast forth | ἐκβάλη | ekbalē | throw out, cast out |

Matthew says that Jesus did not answer her right away, inferring that she continued, so the disciples wanted to send her away.

27 let   ἄφες   aphes   suffer to, allow

The idea here was that Jesus came first to the Jews, but they rejected Him (Jn. 1:11, Ps. 118:22). Jesus was testing her perseverance.

first	πρῶτον	prōton	
be filled	χορτασθῆναι	chortasthēnai	be satisfied
meet	καλὸν	kalon	good, proper
to take	λαβεῖν	labein	to seize in hand
bread	ἄρτον	arton	
dogs	κυναρίοις	kunariois	religious corrupters

The woman did not resent this expression, but accepted it

28
answered	ἀπεκρίθη	apekrithē	respond, reply
dogs	κυνάρια	kunaria	little dogs, household pets
under	ὑποκάτω	hupokatō	beneath, underneath
eat	ἐσθίουσιν	esthiousin	to eat or drink
crumbs	ψιχίων	psichiōn	little scraps of bread

Often children sitting at the table would slip scraps to their pets under the table; so that the dogs would be eating at the same time as the children.

29
for this	διὰ τοῦτον	dia touton	
(your) saying	(τὸν) λὸγον	(ton) logon	
is gone	ἐξελήλυθεν	exelēluthen (exerchomai)	has gone forth

Matthew says that Jesus cited her faith.

30
when she was come	ἀπελθοῦσα	apelthousa	
her house	οἶκον αὐτῆς	oikon autēs	
she found	εὗρεν	heuren (heuriskō)	to find, meet with, detect
laid	βεβλημένον	beblēmenon (ballō)	to throw or cast
bed	κλίνην	klinēn (klinō)	to bow, to lay, couch, bed

Lessons from the lesson:
- Jesus cannot be hid (24).
- Sometimes we must rest in order for our ministry to be effectual (24)

- God's work is not limited or confined to one National boundary (25, 26).
- We must not underestimate demon possession in this modern world and time (26).
- Faith is strengthened by challenge (27).
- Jesus is the bread of life (Jn. 6:48); this woman was the recipient of the children's crumbs (28).
- Distance is no matter to Jesus (29, 30).
- Real faith is persistent (28).
- This woman's faith is a challenge to every Christian (Matt. 15:28).
- Prayer is an effective weapon when attacked by demons (29, 30).
- The healing method is not as important as the healer (30).
- Faith must be tested (27, 28).

True Treasure Costs

Introduction:

This same episode is written in two other gospels; Matthew 19:16-30; and Luke 18:18-30. It is a lesson in habitual, surface, shallow religious practice, rather than the depth of following Jesus completely and thoroughly, beyond the letter.

Translation, transliteration, interpretation:

v.	English	Greek	Transliterated	Alternative meanings
17	good master	διδάσκαλε ἀγαθέ	didaskale agathe	good teacher
	inherit	κληρονομήσω	klēronomēs	to get, to obtain, receive
18	Jesus is attempting to place the young man's attention on Him as God in the flesh.			
19	Jesus is also focusing the attention of the young man, purposely on the 2nd table of the law each relating to relationships with others.			
20	observed	ἐφυλαξάμην	ephulaxamēn	I have kept
	From my youth: this statement refers to the age of 12 years, when Jewish boys received special recognition relating to the Torah.			
	Matthew cites the young man asking "which law?"			
21	beholding	ἐμβλέψας	emblepsas	looking upon, with a glance of affection
	loved	ἠγάπησεν	ēgapēsen (agapē)	(some translators say that Jesus fell in love with this charming youth)
	lackest	ὑστερεῖ	husterei (husteros)	behind, late, come short
	Matthew says the youth asked, "what lack I yet" (19:20)			
	sell	πώλησον	pōlēson (poleō)	to sell
	give	δὸς	dos (didōmi)	present, supply, bestow, give

Matthew 19:21, Jesus says "if thou will be perfect." This word telos means ripe, entire, complete.

treasure	θυσαυρὸν	thusauron	precious deposit, storehouse
come	δεῦρο	deuro	come hither (imperative)
take up	απας	apas (hairō)	take, choose (alt)
Cross	σταυρον	stauron (stauroō)	(alt)
follow	ἀκολούθει	akolouthei	to imitate, follow as a disciple
poor	πτωχοῖς	ptochois	lowly, indigent, beggar, poor
22 went away	ἀπῆλθεν	apēlthen (arerchomai)	depart, go away
sad	στυγνάσας	stugnasas	somber, gloomy
grieved	λυπούμενος	lupoumenos	sorrowful
23 hard	δυσκόλως	duskolōs	with difficulty
24 astonished	ἐθαμβοῦντο	ethambounto	to be amazed
trust	πεποιθοτας	pepoithotas (peithō)	persuasion, influence, hope (alt)
riches	χρήματα	chrēmata (chrematizō)	money, price, wealth
25 needle {	ῥαφίδος	rhaphidos	
	βελόνες	belones	surgical needle (Luke 18:25)
perforation {	τρυμαλιᾶς	trumalias	hole, eye of needle
	τρυπήματος	trupēmatos	hole, eye of needle (Matthew 19:24)
easier	εὐκοπώτερόν	eukopōteron	more feasible
out of measure	περισσῶς	perissōs	extraordinary, exceedingly
28 left	ἀφήκαμεν	afēkamen	to depart, leave behind, alone

Lessons from the lesson:
- Some followers of Jesus still run and kneel down before Him (as the Gadarene) and this man, 17.
- Seeking only to obey the law will never satisfy the soul (19, 20).
- Sinners have a sense that something is missing in their lives (20).
- To truly know Jesus requires complete surrender to Him (21, 22).
- Where a man's treasure is, there will his heart be also (Matt. 6:21, 22).

- Earthly wealth can never satisfy the soul (22).
- The priority of man's trust determines his position in God's Kingdom: first or last (22).
- The failures of others should teach great lessons (23).
- Possession of wealth does not mean that one is living righteously (24).
- Loving God is related with loving others (1Jn. 4:20, 21).
- Religious pretending sooner or later will be exposed (20, 21, 22).
- The delight of God's blessings far exceeds enjoyment of worldliness (30).
- Following Jesus is not just going along with the crowd (20).
- God is well aware of our sacrifices (29, 30).
- Many who suppose themselves to have first place in God's Kingdom will have last place, if at all, (31).
- God is treasurer of heaven (21).
- There must be a Cross in our lives (21).

Elizabeth's Commitment

LUKE 1:39-45

Introduction:

Last week's lesson was about Mary's song of praise; having been chosen by God to be the vessel through which Jesus would be delivered. In today's lesson there is another song of praise; this time being sung by cousin Elizabeth. Her home is believed to have been in Hebron of Judea. Judea is very hilly and mountainous. Mary, coming from Nazareth to visit Elizabeth would have had to travel at least 40 miles. She probably traveled in a caravan going south. It would have been at least a three day journey.

Translation, transliteration, interpretation:

v.	English	Greek	Transliterated	Alternative meanings
39	arose	ἀναστᾶσα	anastasa	

Luke, the writer, is fond of this term. He uses it in his writing some 60 times.

	English	Greek	Transliterated	Alternative meanings
	hill country	ὀπεινὴν	oreinēn (oros)	mountain or hill

Luke writes hill, perhaps meaning mountain. Joshua names the mountains of Judea in 15:4.8-60.

v.	English	Greek	Transliterated	Alternative meanings
40	saluted	ἠσπάσατο	ēspasato (aspazomai)	greet with affection, express good wishes salutation (see salute above)

Mary's first glance at Elizabeth would have confirmed the angel's message of her pregnancy.

v.	English	Greek	Transliterated	Alternative meanings
41	leaped	ἐσκίρτησεν	eskirtēsen (skirtao)	to leap or skip

Both mother and the unborn baby rejoiced together at the news of Jesus.

	English	Greek	Transliterated	Alternative meanings
	filled	ἐπλήσθη	eplēsthē (plethō, pimplēmi)	full influence

v.	English	Greek	Transliterated	Alternative meanings
42	loud	μευάλῇ	megalē	great range, intense
	voice	φωνη	phōnē	(alt): κραυγη, *kraugē*
	blessed	εὐλογημένη	eulogēmenē	to speak well of someone, to invoke a blessing

This would be the first beatitude of the New Testament. The last in the gospels is spoken to Thomas, Jn. 20:29.

In verse 42 Elizabeth begins to sing her song of praise, glory and gratitude.

	fruit	καρπὸς	karpos	offspring, posterity, benefit, profit, reward, action
43	whence	πόθεν	pothen	how
44	joy	ἀγαλλιάσει	hagalliasei	exultation, extreme joy
45	Lord	κυρίου	kuriou	

Here, 'Lord' infers the Fatherhood of God; above (43), 'Lord' infers Jesus, the Son of God.

| 45 | fulfillment | τελείωσις | teleiōsis (telos) | result, full performance, result, closing |

Speaking of songs, Zechariah's song is coming in 1:68-70. These are the first of the NT.

Lessons from the lesson:

- Elizabeth's baby, named John the Baptizer, it seems, couldn't get out quick enough to greet Mary's unborn baby, Jesus (41).
- Fellowship with other saints will strengthen our faith (41).
- Where God is honored, saints are welcome, and receive proper reception (40).
- Others can see God's blessings in us; and our reaction to them (42).
- Elizabeth's husband Zechariah is unable to speak to Mary because of his punishment (1:18-20).
- Those who praise God, praise with loud voices (42).
- We cannot take any credit for God's favour (43).
- Elizabeth is so happy for Mary that she forgets herself (42).
- God keeps His word (1:57, 2:7).
- True piety is not envious (43).
- Gen. 3:6: Eve, thru pride, believed the tempter. Mary, thru humility, believed the angel (1:38).

Theology:

42	mariolatry, (the belief that Mary is God's mother) which is false.
35	incarnation.
1:57, 2:7	miracle.
Phil. 2:7	self emptying.
1:35, 41	Holy Spirit.
1:11, 28	angels.

42	Praise (46-55, 42-45).
45	Lordship of Christ.
45	Lordship of God, prophecy, fulfillment, faith.
44	Joy.

A Life of Total Commitment

LUKE 1:46-55

Introduction:

In the fullness of time, God sent forth His Son, made of a woman, made under the law (Gal. 4:4). Luke spells out for us the details of this virgin birth. It is the fulfillment of Isaiah's prophecy, Isaiah 7:14.

Mary's life was one of total commitment to the Lord.

Commitment:

Gen. 39:8	נָתַן	nā-TAN	to give
Job 5:8	שִׂים	SĪM	to put or place
Ps. 10:14	עָזוּב	ā-ZAV	to leave self to
Jn. 5:22	δίδωμ	didōmi	to give
Acts 27:40	ἐάω	eao	to let be
Rom. 3:2	πιστεύω	pisteuo	to trust, confide
1 Tim. 1:18	παρατίθημι	paratithēmi	to put alongside
1 Pe. 2:23	παραδίδωμι	paradidēmi	to give over

Mary's song of joy here is similar to Hannah's, 1 Sam. 2:1-10.

Translation, transliteration, interpretation:

v.	English	Greek	Transliterated	Alternative meanings
46	magnify	μεγαλύνει	megalunei	to enlarge, amplify, extoll, exalt, glorify
	In the Latin, this is called Mary's Magnificat (song of praise).			
	soul	ψυχή	psuchē	
47	spirit	πνεῦμά	pneuma	
48	regarded	ἐπέβλεψεν	epeblepsen	looked upon
	low estate	ταπείνωσιν	tapeinōsin	humble, poor, lowly, modest, humiliation

Blessed, this same beattitude is used by Elizabeth when Mary visits her (Lk. 1:42, see 11:27).

49	name	ὄνομα	onoma	reputation, representative, possessor of certain character by which the Lord reveals Himself to men
51	proud	ὑπερηφάνους	huperēphanous	haughty

It is said that pride is the parent of sin.

| | scattered | διεσκόρπισεν | dieskorpisen | to disperse |

Arm: the arm represents the greatest strength, the hand a little less, the finger least.

52	put down	καθεῖλεν	kathailen	take down, demolish, destroy, conquer, overthrow; see Luke 10:18 (Satan is cast down)
	exalted	ὕψωσεν	hupsōsen	elevated, lofty, the height of heaven
53	filled	ἐνέπλησεν	eneplēsen	to be satisfied, full
	He sent away	ἐξαπέστειλεν	exapesteilen	to dismiss, dispatch, pervading influence
	empty	κενούς	kenous	hollow, void, empty handed, to no purpose, fruitless
54	holpen	ἀντελάβετο	antelabeto	lay hold of with a view to help, aid, assist, help
	remembrance	μνησθῆναι	mnēsthēnai (mimneskō)	recollect, call to mind impassively

Lessons from the lesson:
- What a blessing, to find favour with God (1:30).
- Faith is singing for joy, while unbelief is silent (46).
- Creatures cannot add to God's greatness (46).
- Mary needed a Saviour too (47).
- To be called "Mother of God" would be blasphemy to Mary, a sinner (47).
- None but believers have a right to rejoice (47) Ecc. 2:2.
- Mary's humility is not celebrated but God's mercy is (48, Mariolatry).
- God often makes something out of nothing (48).
- We should realize that we are blessed (48).
- All sinners are in a low estate (48).
- Everything that God does is great (49).

- God is not only mighty, but He is almighty.
- Holy is only one of God's great names (49).
- A thousand generations is not the full measure of God's mercy (50).
- God's strength is still being demonstrated and will be continually (51).
- The proud are unstable (51).
- Pride overcame the first man and will overcome the last (it feeds in man as a moth).
- The mighty will soon be ejected from their seats (52) Ps. 75:6
- Earth's heights are slippery (Deut. 32:35).
- The saints are journeying from humiliation to exaltation (52).
- God's promises are rich, especially to those who hunger and thirst after righteousness rather than so much for bread (53).

Christ as Teacher

LUKE 4:31-37, 20:1-8

Introduction:

Jesus taught by parable, allegory, simile & metaphor, type and symbol. Not only was His substance effective, but His manner of presenting was impressive. This was the case when He was on earth in the flesh, and it is the case today in the Spirit.

There was a time when Jesus made Capernaum His operating headquarters during His Galilean ministry. He had been rejected at Nazareth, and He was to be rejected here at Capernaum. He will spend some 18 months here. Matthew calls it His own city (9:1). Luke's writing runs parallel with Mark 1:23-28.

Translation, transliteration, interpretation:

v.	English	Greek	Transliterated	Alternative meanings
32	astonished	ἐξεπλήσσοντο	exeplēssonto	to strike out of one's wits, amaze, astound
	power, authority	ἐχουσία	dunamei, echousia	ability, rule, dominion, privilege
33	unclean	ἀκαθάρτου	akathartou	lewd, foul
35	rebuked	ἐπετίμησεν	epetimēsen (epitimaō)	to assess a penalty, reprove, chide, censure, reprimand
	hold thy peace	φιμώθητι	phimōthēti	muzzle, silence, speechless,
	come forth	ἐξῆλθεν	exēlthen (exerchomai)	go, come out of, depart, go away, come forth
	having thrown	ῥῖψαν	rhipsan (rhiptō)	to hurl, cast down, throw, violent gesture
36	astonishment	θάμβος	thambos	awe
37	fame	ἦχος	ēchos	rumour
20:1	came upon	ἐπέστησαν	epestēsan (ephistēmi)	stood up against, sudden appearance

The officials had been planning this action (19:47).

Lessons from the lesson:

- The word of the Lord is astonishing (32).
- The devil recognizes Jesus (34) and us (Acts 19:15).
- The devil and Jesus have nothing in common (34).
- The devil has a seat in the Lord's house (33).
- Heaven, earth, and Satan all meet in God's house (33).
- The devil possesses some pew holders (33).
- Some sacred people attract demons; and some repel them (33).
- Here is the testimony of a demon: confession, knew Jesus, Jesus is Holy, he's in subjection, His judgement is coming (34).
- The devil tares but he must come out at the Lord's command (35).
- Jesus speaks as law maker; not just as an interpreter (36).
- The kind of sin that Satan encourages is unclean (33).
- The demons want Jesus to let them alone, but they won't let us alone (34).
- The demons thought that judgement had come early (34).
- There is a oneness between the devil and the wicked (those that he possesses) (34).
- Here, the devil no longer says if thou be the Son of God (34).
- The devil hates to lose his grasp (35).
- The devil is too weak to resist Jesus' command (35).
- Unsanctified wisdom is dangerous (20:21, 22).
- The wicked will try to rule or ruin those who resist them (20:1).
- These officials pretended to judge Jesus' mission, but couldn't tell that of John (20:2, 7).
- Perhaps they could tell but didn't want to (20:7).
- Enough testimony has been given already to describe Jesus' authority (20:2).
- Those who don't recognize Jesus' miracles will not respect His word & vice versa (20:2).

Suffering and Death

LUKE 23:32-46

Introduction:

In today's lesson we have a panoramic view of God's expression of love; man's expression of sin; and nature's expression of gloom; by virture of the crucifixion of our Lord Jesus Christ.

All of this took place outside the city of Jerusalem (Num. 15:35; Acts 7:58).

Translation, transliteration, interpretation:

v.	English	Greek	Transliterated	Alternative meanings
32	malefactor	κακοῦργοι	kakourgoi	(kakon: evil + ergon: worker) see 2 Tim. 2:9

'Two other' means that Jesus had been identified or accused an evil worker.

	English	Greek	Transliterated	Alternative meanings
	to be put to death	ἀναιρεθῆναι	anairethēnai	take up, take away to kill
33	Calvary	Κρανίον	kranion	skull (Matt. 27:33; Mk. 15:22)

This indeed was a hill that resembled a skull; with openings in the rock for eyes, nose & mouth.

	English	Greek	Transliterated	Alternative meanings
34	forgive	ἄφες	aphes	send away, dismiss, suffer to depart

Jesus preached forgiveness; here He's practicing it. See Isaiah. 50:6, 53:4-7; Ps. 22:1, 6-8, 16-18; Ps. 69:21; Dan. 9:26; Zech. 13:7.

Jesus prayed for His enemies (Heb. 7:25: He made intercession for the transgressors). He, during His ministry, had been during the forgiving; now, as a suppliant, submits to God.

Ignorance is no excuse for transgression; sin is sin to God, whether the sinner knows or not (Num. 15:22-25).

	English	Greek	Transliterated	Alternative meanings
	know not	οἴδασιν	oidasin (oidō)	to know (Acts 3:17; 1 Cor. 2:8)
	parted	διαμεριζόμενοι	diamerizomenoi	to divide into parts and distribute
	cast lots	ἔβαλον	ebalon	threw

	dice	κλήρους	klerous	dice used to determine chances (Matt. 27:35; Ps. 22:18)
35	deride	ἐξεμυκτήριζον	exemuktērizon (mukter)	nose
	He saved	ἔσωσεν	esōsen (sōzō)	(Mark. 15:31; Matt. 27:42)
	chosen	ἐκλεκτός	eklektos (eklegō)	choose, select
36	mock	ἐνέπαιξαν	enepaixan (empaizō)	play upon, deride, scorn, scoff
	vinegar	ὄξος	oxos	a beverage mixed with green herbs to stupify criminal's pain (Matt. 27:34, 48; Mk. 15:36; Lk. 23:36; Jn. 19:29, 30)
37	king	βασιλεὺς	basileus	regal authority
38	title	ἐπιγραφὴ	epigraphē	superscription, γραφω, graphō, to write
39	railed	ἐβλασφήμει	eblasphēmei (blasphēmeō)	revile, irreverence, reproach
40	rebuke	ἐπιτιμῶν	epitimōn (epitimaō)	hide, reprove, set a value upon
	fear	φοβῇ	phobē	
	condemnation	κρίματι	krimati (krinō)	execute, judgement, call to account, try
41	justly,	δικαίως	dikaios, (dikē)	vengence, justice, right
	amiss	ἄτοπον	atopon	out of place (Lk. 23:44; Acts 28:6; 2 Thess. 3:2)
42	remember	μνέσθητι	mnesthēti	
43	verily	ἀμήν	amen	
	paradise	παραδείσῳ	paradeisō	enclosed park, pleasure ground (2 Cor. 12:4; Rev. 2:7)
44	darkness	σκότος	skotos	

This was not an eclipse; the moon being in full on passover night.

46	commend	παρατίθεμαι	paratithemai	to place by the side of, lay before, deposit, to commit, entrust

Ps 31:5

gave up	παρεδωκεν	paredōken	
breath out	ἐξέπνευσεν	exekpneusen	expire

The person to whom Jesus committed His Spirit was His Father.

The spirit of man, distinguished from beast is his link to God (Ecc. 12:7).

Jesus was in the hands of men; here He entrusts- Himself to the Father's care. 3 days later the Father raises Him; 40 days after that, the Father exalts Him.

The Father's hands are a place of eternal security. The heart's true heaven.

Lessons from the lesson:
- Consider the gospel from the enemy:
- "That just man," "Son of God," "He saved others," "King of the Jews," "your Kingdom," "Lord," "was dead" (Jn. 19:33).
- Consider the testimony of nature:
- The veil tore into, darkness covered the earth, the earth quaked, rocks were rent, sun was veiled graves were opened.
- If Jesus prayed for His enemies, what about us (34)?
- No one is beyond the reach of prayer (34).
- Long before we believed in Jesus, He prayed for us.
- Christians are forgiving people.
- Jesus could not save Himself if He was going to save others.
- Jesus practiced what He preached (34): a perfect example.
- The spiritually blind cannot see/understand God's workings (35-37).
- God reveals truth in many ways; sometimes by unlikely means (38).
- Unrepentant sinners make demands of God; repentant ones make requests (39-42).
- True repentance is never unforgiven (43).
- Jesus was born to die (Jn. 12:27, Ps. 41).

Theologically:
- Godhead, Holy Spirit, imputation, propitiation, reconciliation, mediation, redemption, salvation, resurrection, ransom, intercession, substitution, fatherhood, sonship etc.

Resurrected to New Life

LUKE 24:1-12

Introduction:

Jesus had come into the world to be sacrificed for propitiation to God, and imputation to man: He was not surprised being arrested and ultimately crucified. It is interesting that He had foretold His disciples of this event several times and they paid no attention (Matt. 20:19, 16:21; Mk. 10:31-34; Luke 9:22, 18:33, 13:32, 24:7).

Resurrection, (Greek: anastasis), means a standing or a rising up.

Translation, transliteration, interpretation:

v.	English	Greek	Transliterated	Alternative meanings
1	very early	ὄρθου βαθέως	orthou batheōs	early dawn

Obviously, it must have been dark when these women started out. The Sabbath day had ended. The first day of the week had begun at 6pm earlier.

| | sepulchre | μνῆμα | mnēma | grave/tomb; also, קְבוּרָה (qə-vū-RĀH), ταφος, taphos, burning place |
| | spices | ἀρώματα | arōmata | |

Perhaps this was myrrh and aloe as Nicodemus had used earlier (Jn. 19:39-40). The women had observed (Lk. 23:55, 56). The women had prepared spices before the Sabbath to be used after the Sabbath.

| | prepare | ἠτοίμασαν | hētoimasan | ready, make ready |

The women knew about the stone, but didn't know about the guards (Matt. 27:62-66, Mk. 16:3).

3	entered in	εἰσελθοῦσαι	eiserlthousai	to go or come in
	found not	οὐχ εὗρον	ouch heuron	not found
4	perplexed	διαπορεῖσθαι	daiporeisthai	in doubt, utterly at a loss, perplexed (alt)
	shining	ἀστραπτοθση	astraptothse	to be bright, as lightening
5	bowed down to the earth	κλινουσῶν	klinousōn	to bend, to bow down

These women were afraid to look up at the angels.

		seek	ζητεῖτε	zēteite,	look for, search after, strive
		among	μετὰ	meta	together with
6		how He spake	ἐλάλησεν	elalēsen (laleō)	to talk, to speak to

The third day, this is believed to be a trope or figure of speech; where a whole is given for a part, or a part is given for a whole, as in Lk. 2:1: "whole world" was not the whole world but a part of the world (this is controversial, since Jesus used the term).

7	be delivered	παραδοθῆναι	paradothēnai	
	hands	χεῖρας	cheiras	by agency
8	remember	ἐμνήσθησαν	emnēsthēsan (mimnskō)	call to mind, recollect
	words	ῥημάτων	rhematōn (rheō)	to say, speak, address
9	returned	ὑποστρέψασαι	hupostrepsasa	to turn back to
	the rest	λοιτοῖς	loitois	to be left
11	idle tales	λῆρος	leros	idle talk, empty tales
	seemed	ἠπίστουν	epistoun	want of trust, violation of faith
12	ran	ἔδραμεν	edramen (trechō)	advance, progress freely, advance rapidly
	beheld	βλέπει	blepei	exercise sight
	laid	κειμενα	keimena	having been lain down, be lying, be situated

Lessons from the lesson:

- There were six Marys in Jesus' life:
- Jesus' mother (Matt. 1:16).
- Mother of James the Less and Joses (Matt. 27:56, 61).
- The sister of Martha (Jn. 12:3; Lk. 10:39, 42; Jn. 11:2).
- Mary Magdalene (Matt. 15:39).
- The mother of John Mark (Acts 12:12).
- There was a rush to get the bodies down from the Crosses, as the Sabbath was approaching (Jn. 19 31-33).
- It was not Jesus's friends that pronounced His death but the soldiers. This should end the theory that Jesus was not dead.
- Since Jesus has risen, spices must take a different form (1).
- The stone represented many obstacles that prevent men from seeing God's revelation (2).

- The empty tomb contained much revelation (3, 12).
- God's messenger is always just in time (4).
- Remembering things in the past that we paid no attention to is of great importance (5).
- Truth is often difficult to believe; only by faith (Jn. 20:29).
- Along with God's revelation comes responsibility (8, 9, Lk.12:48).
- New truth should be weighed thoroughly and compared with old truth (12).
- Seeing the place where Jesus was is good; but seeing Jesus is better (Lk. 24:36).

Things to think about:
- Unused spices
- Empty tomb
- Missing body
- Torn veil
- Open graves
- Missing bodies of saints
- 40 days after the resurrection
- 50 days after the resurrection.

Witness to Life

LK. 24:44-53

Introduction:

In this lesson we will see the closing days of Jesus' humanity on earth with His disciples, and the beginning of His humanity in heaven. We will see the importance of the Scriptures, and the believers' understanding and use of them. We will see the proper spiritual energetic exertion and physical response to Jesus' command.

v.	English	Greek	Transliterated	Alternative meanings
44	fulfilled	πληρωθῶναι	plērōthōnai	wholly occupied, completely under influence of

The law, the prophets, and the hagiographa are the three divisions of the Hebrew Bible.

v.	English	Greek	Transliterated	Alternative meanings
45	understanding	νοῦν	noun	mind, intellect, thought, concept
	opened	διήνοιχεν	diēvoichen	to open the sense of a thing, open the mind or heart
46	behoved	ἐδει	edei	to bind, confine, impede, impel, compel
	rise	ἀναστῆναι	anastēnai	cause to stand, rise up into existence, resurrection
47	repentance	μετάνοιαν	metanoian	a change of mind, principle, practice remission
	remission	ἄφεσιν	aphesin	to dismiss, suffer to depart, expire
48	witness	μάρτυρες	martures	a witness to a circumstance, a testifier
49	promise	ἐπαγγλίαν	epagglian	declare, announce, annunciation
	endued		evdusēsthe	clothe, invested, array, envelope

109

power	δύναμιν	dunamin	strength, ability, efficacy, authority, energy
50	Bethany was known as the House of Dates. It was adjoining the Mount of Olives (Mk. 11:1, Lk. 19:29, Jn. 11:18), near the place where Jesus prayed for Jerusalem.		
51 blessed	εὐλογεῖν	eulogein	to speak well of, ascribe praise
carried up	ἀναφέρετο	avaphereto	lead up, to bear, carry upwards
52 worship	προσκυνήσαντες	proskunēsantes	to do reverence or homage

Lessons from the lesson:
- All of the figures had to be explained and understood: simile, type, parable, symbol, metaphor, allegory, etc (44).
- Jesus is the fulfillment of the scriptures (which are Christocentric, 44).
- God put His revelation in writing (44).
- Words are only words without understanding (which comes from the Lord, 45).
- Jesus had to suffer, die, be raised, and ascend for us (it behoved Him, 46).
- The Lord's plan is that all men and Nations be aware of salvation and forgiveness of sin (47).
- All who know Christ are witnesses (they have seen, heard, felt and experienced something, 48).
- Christians must learn to wait; (as Abraham, Moses, the hemorrhaging woman (12 years), 1 Jn. 1:1-3, the man of Bethesda (38yrs), and as the disciples).
- Repentance of sin is man's act; remission of sin is God's; they must be preached together (47).
- Power of the saints comes from on high; from our God (49, Acts 1:8).
- Joy and praise follows worship and causes worship (53).
- God shows as much power and love in bringing men to Jesus as in sending Jesus to men.

Christ as Servant

JOHN 13:1-8, 12-20

Introduction:

Today we see Christ as servant. He came, not to be ministered to, but to minister (Matt. 20:28). Our charge is to follow His example by serving our fellow man; for in doing so, we are serving Him.

Translation, transliteration, interpretation:

v.	English	Greek	Transliterated	Alternative meanings
1	knew	εἰδὼς	eidōs	full consciousness

With respect to Christ, He is omniscient, already knowing, not needing to learn. The word "know" is in our lesson 6 times, vs. 1, 3, 7, 7, 12, 17.

	English	Greek	Transliterated	Alternative meanings
	unto	εἰς	eis	to the uttermost
	hour	ὥρα	hōra	appointed time
	should depart	μεταβῇ	metabē	to go from one place to another

His own (those He had chosen).

v.	English	Greek	Transliterated	Alternative meanings
2	being ended	γινομένου	ginomenou	

From vs. 4, 12 we see that the meal was yet going on. It is more properly translated, "during the supper."

	English	Greek	Transliterated	Alternative meanings
	having put	βεβληκότος	beblēkotos (ballō)	to cast, to put
	betray	παραδοῖ	paradoi	to deliver up (Mark 14:10)
3	had given	ἔδωκεν	edōken (didōmi)	bestow, supply, present
4	lays aside	τίθησιν	tithēsin (tithēmi)	to set, place, put off
	He girded	διέζωσεν	diezōsen (diazōnnuō)	gird firmly around
	garments	ἱμάτια	himatia	outer robe (iallith). His tunic remained on Him.
5	basin	νιπτῆρα	niptēra (nizō)	a wide shallow bowl from which to wash a person's parts
7	hereafter	μετὰ ταῦτα	meta tauta	
8	never	οὐ μὴ	ou mē	in no wise
	forever	εἰς τὸν αἰῶνα	eis ton aiōna	

	part	μέρος	meros	division of a whole
10	but not all (a reference to Judas, who is still there).			
14	ought	ὀφείλετε	opheilete	to owe a debt (Matt. 18:30)
15	example	ὑπόδειγμα	hupodeigma (hupodeiknumi)	token, indicate, intimation
16	greater	μείζων	meizōn	(the comparative degree)
17	know	οἴδατε	oidate	regard with favour
	ye do	ποιῆτε	poiēte (poieō)	keep on doing
18	heel	πτέρναν	pternan	with which to trip or kick in wrestling
19	before it comes	πρὸ του γενέσθαι	pro tou genesthai	
	when it comes to pass	ὅταν γένηται	hotan genētai	whenever

Lessons from the lesson:
- Here we have Christ's unchanging love; and Judas' unchanging hatred (1, 2).
- Jesus was never taken by surprise (2).
- Jesus, one year previously, had seen that Judas was demon possessed (Jn. 6:70).
- Satan had an open door to the heart of Judas; and great access to the heart of sinners (2).
- Satan went into the heart of Judas when he offered to betray Jesus (Lk. 22:3).
- Jesus looked beyond the Cross (3).
- Christ is the laver of the Temple from which we are washed (5).
- The feet of the apostles were washed; the feet of Jesus were anointed (12:3).
- Our feet will best be placed in the hands of the Lord (8).
- There are those who think to be better morally even than the Lord (8).
- Peter was impulsive, even in his humility (8).
- The first condition of discipleship is surrender (8).
- Jesus is waiting for man with the basin in His hand (5).
- Cleaning of the dirt of sin is a daily necessity (12).
- Here is a breach of hostility; to eat someone's food, and then turn on them (10, 2, 18) (Ps. 41:9).
- It's one thing to call Jesus Lord & Master; but another thing to follow Him (13).
- A Godly status does not exempt from service (15).
- Serving others brings joy to the server (17).
- Only knowing does not bring happiness, nor does occasional doing (17).

- Blood affects out standing; water affects our state.
- Blood is judicial; water is practical & experiential.
- Blood is expiational; water is purificational.
- Blood saves; water washes.

Discerning Gifts for Leaders

ACTS 6:1-5, 8-15

Introduction:

In our lesson today, we will see that the more people added to the early Church, the more problems it had. We will see that the Church began to have varying troubles both inside and out. The Holy Spirit has His way of solving both kinds of problems.

Translation, transliteration, interpretation:

v.	English	Greek	Transliterated	Alternative meanings
1	multiplied	πληθυνόντων	plēthunontōn	fullness, to increase, was multiplying

Many people were still in town from the observance of the Feast of Pentecost. The Grecian Jews were called Hellenists because they were acculturated in Grecian cities.

	English	Greek	Transliterated	Alternative meanings
	murmuring	γογγυσμὸς	goggusmos	to mutter, murmur, secret grumbling (until heard)
	were neglected	παρεθεωροῦντο	paretheōrounto	to look beyond, to overlook
	ministration	διακονία	diakonia	a serving or a service
2	not reason	οὐκ ἀπεστόν	ouk apeston	not seemly, not proper, unacceptable, not pleasing
3	look ye out	ἐπισκέψασθε	episkepsasthe	inspect, select, look at observantly, appoint

The apostles were capable of picking out worthy persons, but they desired to include the people.

	English	Greek	Transliterated	Alternative meanings
4	give ourselves	προσκαρτερήσομεν	proskarterēsomen	persist in adherence, intently engage in

5 It is interesting to observe that the congregation selected 7 Grecian men; 2 of whom eventually became evangelists.

8	full	πλήρες	plēres	wholly occupied with, abounding in, completely under influence of
	wonders	τέρατα	terata	great astounding acts
	miracles	σημεῖα	sēmeia	sign, proof, wonderful work
	there arose	ἀνέστησαν	anestēsan	stood up
9	disputing	συζητοῦντες	suzētountes	to debate, argue, question

Here were 5 kinds of Synagogues out of the many in Jerusalem. Schurer calls the number of 480 Synagogues in the city a Talmudic myth.

Libertines were freed Jewish prisoners from Rome; having been captured by Pompey in Syrian war.

Cyrenians were Hellenist Jews, having lived in Greek cities (Libya).

Alexandrians were a Jewish colony, having been given citizenship from Egypt.

Cilicians were Jews from Paul's country. Perhaps he engaged in the debate, as in the stoning.

Asians were from a Roman province where Ephesus was the capital.

Pontius Pilate was still Govenor; Caiaphas the High Priest, and Tiberius the Emperor.

The same charges were leveled against Jesus: blaspheming against the law, God, and the Temple.

10	resist	ἀνιστῆναι	anistēmai	opposition, stand out against
11	suborned	ὑπέβαλον	hupebalon	put under as a rug, bring men under control, by suggestion or money
12	stirred up	συνεκίνησάν (συγκῑνέω)	sunekinēsan (sugkineō)	shook people together as an earthquake, throw into commotion
	caught Him	συνήρπασαν (συναρπάζω)	sunērpasan (sunērpazō)	seized as if after pursuit
13	false witnesses	μάρτυρας ψευδεῖς	marturas pseudeis	
14	customs	ἔθη	ethē	

| 15 | face | πρόσωπον | prosōpon | as they saw the face of Moses (Ex. 34:30, 2 Cor. 3:7) |

Perhaps Paul told Luke (the writer) about this detail.
Jesus had spoken of the destruction of two Temples: Jn. 2:19; Mk. 13:1, 2.

Lessons from the lesson:
- In the Church there were inside murmurings and outside disputes (1, 9).
- God provides the solutions (3, 10).
- Often the so-called needs of parishioners are not genuine (1).
- The Word of God should not be neglected for any reason (2) neither the needs of the saints.
- God's Word is more important than serving tables; He is the origin of the table (2).
- The Holy Ghost guides both the congregation and the pastor (3-5).
- Preaching God's Word is a continuing duty, and must be accompanied by prayer (4).
- The Deacons may serve physical alms, but the preachers serve spiritual food, God's Word (4).
- Christians should have irresistible knowledge, spirit, and wisdom as Stephen did (5).
- Deacons must be qualified to serve, as well as the preacher (3).
- With spiritual progress often comes opposition (9).
- Wisdom is one of the gifts of the spirit (10).
- Jesus was seen standing when Stephen was stoned (15).
- Pastors often have to do things that others could do (4).
- The poor are God's business and should be ours (3).
- Men ought always pray (4).

A New Beginning for Saul

ACTS 9:1-11, 16-19

Introduction:

In this story of the conversion of Saul, the Hebrew Pharasee, the persecutor becomes the persecuted; the enemy becomes a friend, and an opposer is opposed. The fearful saints receive assurance, and God is glorified.

After the taste of blood from Stephen, Saul begins to fulfill the prophecy of his forefather Jacob (Gen. 49:27). He has become a ravine wolf. He is exhaling and inhaling cruelty to the saints. Damascus is 150 miles away from Jerusalem. He, being a Pharisee has obtained authority from Caiaphas (who is a Sadducee and Chief Priest in charge of the Hebrew worship of the region) to go to Damascus and search out Christians for persecution (sort of a Federal Bureau of Investigation). The name Saul is Aramaic. It seems that Saul's request was sort of a favour to himself.

Translation, transliteration, interpretation:

v.	English	Greek	Transliterated	Alternative meanings
1	breathing out	ἐμπνεών	empneōn	to be animated with the spirit of
	threatening	ἀπειλῆς	apeilēs	harshness of language
	slaughter	φόνου	phonon	killing, murder
2	the way	τῆς ὁδοῦ	tēs hodou	conduct, course of action, system of doctrine
	bound	δεδεμένους	dedemenous (deō)	bind, confine, hinder, prohibit
3	came near	ἐγγίζειν	eggizein (eggus)	close at hand, impending
4	persecutest	διώκεις	diōkeis	pursue with malignity
	kick	λακτίζειν	laktizein (lax)	with the heel
	pricks	κέντρα	kentra	sharp pointed stick to sting or goad animals

These two terms above come from Paul's account of his conversion in Acts 26:14.

6	astonished	θαμβων	thambōn	amazement, awe struck (alt)
11	enquire	ζήτησον	zētēson (zeteō)	seek, look for, strive for

Saul had surrendered, as Thomas had done after seeing the risen Jesus.

The name Ananias means 'God is gracious.'

Saul no doubt had prayed before, but never in a situation like this.

18	scales	λεπίδες	lepides	shell, rind, crust
	forthwith	παραψρημα	parachrēma	immediately

Lessons from the lesson:

- Saul never forgot this experience (9:3-18, 22:6-16, 26:12-20); this seeing and sending of Christ qualified Saul to be an apostle (Gal. 1:16; 1 Cor. 15:8).
- Sometimes threatenings from enemies of Christ come with every breath (1).
- It's strange that men use the same breath that God gives them to curse and blaspheme Him.
- Travelers on "the way" of Christ were hard to find then, and they are hard to find today (2).
- The cruelist sinner is no match for the convicting work of the Lord (3-5).
- The light of Christ is strong enough to knock a sinner down (3).
- Persecuting of the saints is persecuting their Lord (1, 2, 4).
- Saul didn't choose Christ, it was Christ who chose him (3) Gal. 1:15.
- Kicking and resisting the Lord only hurts the kicker (5).
- A new Christian needs an experienced one for strength, guidance, and example (6, 10, 11).
- The power of the Lord can make saints out of sinners (5).
- Open eyes are not always seeing eyes (8).
- There are some things that sinners must do in order to comply with the will of God (6).
- Saul's message was personal; those traveling with him didn't get the message (7).
- You can always find God's saints on Straight Street (11).
- There is suffering in sainthood (16).
- Jesus must be properly described (17).

Grace in Times of Trouble

2 COR. 11:17, 21-30; 12:9, 10

Introduction:

Regarding this epistle, there are some who think that Paul had inferred writing one or two more letters to this Church (1 Cor. 5:9; 2 Cor. 2:1-3).

Paul had many concerns regarding this Church: regarding the poor saints at Jerusalem, this Church had promised financial support and was very slow fulfilling it.

They were allowing and following false teachers (11:3, 4). Paul speaks here of another Jesus, another gospel, and another Spirit which they were endorsing.

There were false charges that Paul was not genuine.

Paul mentions that he had robbed other Churches for them, ἐσύλησα, *esulēsa*, (stripped from a slain foe) meaning that he had allowed other Churches to do more than their share.

2 Cor. 11:8: taking wages, ὀψώνιον, opsonion, meaning that he had received his rations from other Churches rather than Corinth.

11:16: Here Paul may have appeared or sounded foolish, but didn't want to be called foolish.

10:1: He had just appealed to the example of Christ and didn't want to appear contradictory.

On their part, there was self inflation, self commendation, and self indulgence; but on Paul's part was self authentication.

v.	English	Greek	Transliterated	Alternative meanings
17	Here Paul uses a disclaimer (speaking not as from the Lord).			
21	reproach	ἀτιμίαν	atimian	extensive irony presented as charge of another

They tolerated others to trample, but criticized the weak who were being trampled on.

After this, Paul changes the tone from irony to direct assertion.

Where others speak of boasting (being robbers of His liberty), I will use your method to make my point. I will lower myself to speak your language (vs. 18).

	bold	τολμῶ κἀγώ	tolmō kagō	real courage

The Corinthians were impressed with these false teachers.

22 Paul's detractors were Hebrews, legalistic Judiazers (Acts 15:1; Gal. 2:16). Paul also was a Hebrew; but he counted his gain as losses (Phil. 3:5, 7).

23 Paul says that if the test of being a servant of Christ was sacrifice, he had more than passed the test (1 Cor. 15:10), he had laboured more than they all.

I speak as a fool (23-27).

26 perils   κινδύνοις   kindunois   dangers

Perils, meaning dangers (all of his perils, are not listed, many being incurred after this epistle, around 55 A.D.).

He was beaten with sticks at Philippi, stoned at Lystra, (see Deut. 25:3, Acts16:22, 23; 14:19), at

Lystra, assumed dead; this may have been the time of his being caught up in paradise.

Lessons from the lesson:

- Boasting is a mark of folly (17).
- We have nothing which we have not received (21), Rom. 7:18; 1 Cor. 4:7.
- In our flesh dwelleth no good thing (Phil. 3:3: we should have no confidence in the flesh).
- Self centeredness is not Godly; but fleshly (17).
- Boasting comes natural to the ungodly (16, 17, 21-22).
- False teachers are inspired by Satan (13, 14).
- Paul's suffering should shame us (23-30).
- True believers have difficulties also (23-30).
- Troubles do not mean we are not Christians.
- Persecution is evidence of the faithfulness, or provocation for it (22, 23).
- We are often unaware of many of the burdens that Church leaders bear (28, 29); pray for them.
- God blesses us in spite of ourselves (30).
- God demonstrates His power in our weakness (10).
- Trials are blessings because they lead to triumphs (12:11).
- Human weakness opens the way for more of Christ's grace and power (10).
- Paul's enemies had a hard time making him unhappy by persecution (10).

Confronting Opposition

GAL. 2:11-21

Introduction:

The Churches of Galatia included cities of Lystra, Iconium, Derby, and Antioch (Acts 14). Some of the opposition came from unbelieving Jews (14:2, 19; 15:2). Other forms of opposition came from believing Jews who had false beliefs about Jesus and salvation (15:1, 13:45).

Paul preached the same gospel to the Jews as he did to the Gentiles (2). False teachers were imported to spy on Pauls team and make accusations against them (4) this was the "other gospel" that Paul warned the Galatians against (1:6-9).

Peter had already preached to the Gentiles, in the person of Cornelius (Acts 11:11-18). Paul and Barnabus were also preaching to the Gentiles (Acts 13:46-48).

James, the pastor of the Jerusalem Church sent men back to Antioch with Paul and Barnabus (Acts 15:22-27). Meanwhile, Peter had been fellowshipping with the Gentiles at Antioch. When Paul arrived with the men from Jerusalem, Peter pretended not to fellowship with the Gentiles. This was definitely wrong (Gal. 3:26-29).

Translation, transliteration, interpretation:

v.	English	Greek	Transliterated	Alternative meanings
11	withstood	ἀντέστην	antestēn (anthistēmi)	to resist, to stand against
	Peter's reputation was at stake with the other Jews.			
	to be blamed	κατεγνωσμένος	kategnōsmenos	to be condemned, to stand condemned
13	dissembled	συνυπεκρίθησαν	sunupekrithēsan	to pretend to, act a part with, hide one's feelings
	was carried away	συναπήχθη	sunapēchthē (sunapagō)	lead away, carry astray
	Even Barnabas was carried away with this kind of attitude.			
	dissimulation	ὑποκρίσει	hupokrisei	hypocrisy, not merely acting but being

14	uprightly	ὀρθοποδοῦσιν (orthopodeō)	orthopodousin	orthos = straight, pous = foot: to walk straight.

16 Justification is the judicial act of God as judge, whereby He declares righteous, those who have accepted Jesus.

		δικαιοῦται (dikaioō, dike)	dikaioutai	declare righteous, Make worthy
18	transgressor	παραβάτην	parabatēn	to over step
21	frustrate	ἀθετῶ	athetō	to set aside, make void, make ineffective

Lessons from the lesson:

- Our reputation with men may be at stake, living a Christian life, but our soul is at stake with God (11).
- Fearing people more than fearing God leads to compromise (11).
- It takes courage to deal with our people (11).
- God is holding each of us accountable for our example (12-14).
- Rebuking our brothers and sisters, when in the wrong, is proof of our love for them (14).
- If we live like sinners, why compel them to be Christians (14)?
- Justification with God is not by works (16).
- Prejudice is sin (18).
- Jewish rituals are not binding on Christians (16).
- Faith is our response to God's grace; with repentance (16).
- Salvation is not earned or merited, but God's gift to the Godly (Rom. 6:23, 16:26).
- Christ died for our sins and was raised for our justification (1 Cor. 15:3; Rom. 4:23).
- If we have been freed from the law which condemns, through Christ, how can we continue to live in it (20, 21)?
- Through Christ the Mosiac law was abolished (Col. 2:14).
- Justification of God will not lead people into more sin but less (16, Heb. 8:7-13).
- Many frustrate the grace of God, by resisting it, keeping it from having its intended effect (21).

New Relation in Christ

EPH. 3:1-13

Introduction:

Here we have yet another lesson from the epistle of Paul, the apostle of the Lord. This letter is impersonal. Perhaps there are now members of the Church whom he has never met. This letter is not about his imprisonment or persecution, but about God's purpose in Christ. Paul is not now writing especially to the local Church, but to the one Universal Church.

Translation, transliteration, interpretation:

v.	English	Greek	Transliterated	Alternative meanings
1	prisoner	δέσμιος	desmios (deō)	to bind, impede, hinder
	Gentiles	ἐθνῶν	ethnōn	Nations
2	(surely) you have heard: dispensation of grace (see Col. 1:25)			
3	revelation	ἀποκάλθψιν	apokalupsin	to reveal, manifest, declare
	mystery	μυστήριον	musterion (mueō)	to shut the mouth, a secret, concealed, hidden
4	understand	σύνεσίν	sunesin	perception

Paul's special knowledge gives Him a special claim to speak of the mysteries of Christ.

	my knowledge	νοῆσαι	noēsai (noeō, nous)	mind, intellect, opinion, judgement
5	was not made known	οὐκ ἐγνωπίσθη	ouk egnōristhē	

God's purpose is not new, but its manifestation is (see Romans 16:25).

'Apostles and prophets' see Col. 2:20, the Church, having been built on their foundation.

The Church's dim light was like darkness compared with the day of new revelation.

| 6 | fellow heirs | συγκληρονόμα | sugklēronoma | joint heirs |

	same body	σύσσωμα	sussēma (sussēmos)	a joint body
	partakers	συμμέτοχα	summetocha (summetochos)	joint partakers (of a house)
7	minister	διάκονος	diakonos	servant
8	unsearchable	ἀνεξιχνίαστον	anexichniaston	ex = out + ichnos to track = to track out, unexplorable
9	make all men see	φωτίσαι	phōtisai (phatizō)	to turn the light on, to enlighten
	fellowship	κοινωνια	koinōnia (koines)	sharer, partaker, associate
10	intent	γνωρισθῇ	gnōristhē (ginoskō, gnorizō)	purpose
	principalities	ἀρχαῖς	archais (archē)	extremity, headship, authority, high estate
	manifold	πολυποίκιλος	polupoikilos	with many colours, varied, multifarious
11	purpose	πρόθεσιν	prothesin (protithēmi)	to determine, design beforehand
12	boldness	μαρρησίαν	parrēsian	openness, freedom in speaking, frankness (see 2:18)
	confidence	πεποιθήσει	pepoithēsei (pepoitha, peithō)	convince, influence, persuade
13	faint	ἐγκακεῖν	egkakein	give in to, behave badly; kakos, bad

Lessons from the lesson:
- Saints are voluntary prisoners of Christ.
- Ours are the dispensations; God is the dispenser. (2).
- God has uncovered many mysteries to us without which we would still be in the dark (3).
- Christ is the newest and highest revelation (3).
- We must read God's Word for a greater understanding, not having to rely on oral tradition (4).
- Every preacher's sermon reveals the preacher's grasp of the mystery of Christ (4).

- No insight often reveals no call (4).
- God's Holy Spirit makes Holy apostles and prophets (5).
- We are fellow heirs and partakers of the promises of Christ; the gospel is the medium of Christ to His elect (6).
- God's grace is an undeserving gift, and a demonstration of His power (7).
- God's riches of grace are infinite (8).
- God's eternal purpose has been revealed for all to see and know; in His time and on His terms (9, 10, 11).
- God's workings are not always known before time, or during the time (9).
- Once light has been turned on for us, we then can turn it on for others (9).
- God's wisdom is manifold; who can deny it (10)?
- Our boldness and access to God is in Christ (12).
- Many who have suffered and were suffering for God's glory are not suffering to their own shame (13).

Theology:

1 Jesus Christ, Gentiles.
2 Dispensation, grace, God.
3 Revelation, mystery, epistle.
4 Knowledge, understanding.
5 The ages, holiness, apostles, prophets, Holy Spirit.
9 Minister, gift, power.
6 Heirs, gospel, body of Christ, promise.
8 Saints, preach.
9 Fellowship, beginning, world, Creation.
10 Principalities, heaven, Church, wisdom.
11 Eternity, God's purpose, Lord.
12 Faith.
13 Tribulation, glory.

Using Your Gifts

EPH. 4:1-16

Introduction:

Our Lord Jesus, through His Spirit, has given each of His servants, gifts through which to serve Him better, for His glory. Gifts are ministries (1 Cor. 12:3-21).

Paul, the apostle is in prison at Rome, and is writing to the Church which he founded at Ephesus. The letter was delivered by Tychicus with the letter to Colossians and Philemon. It may have been written to the Laodiceans as well (Col. 4:16).

In this chapter he talks about the believer's walk and service (4:1-5:17).

Translation, transliteration, interpretation:

v.	English	Greek	Transliterated	Alternative meanings
1	prisoner	δέσμιος	desmios	(Lk. 8:29, Matt. 27:15, Acts 16:26)

Paul was indeed a prisoner at Rome; but also, a prisoner of the Lord; having been captured (apprehended) by the Lord Jesus (Phil. 3:12).

	English	Greek	Transliterated	Alternative meanings
	beseech	παρακαλῶ	parakalō	to beg, implore, call upon
	vocation	κλήσεως	klēseōs	to invite, calling
	calling	ἐκλήθητε	eklēthēte	to call
2	fore-bearing	ἀνεχόμενοι	anechomenoi	endure patiently, bear with, tolerate, suffer
3	unity	ἑνότητα	henotēta	oneness
	bond	συνδέσμῳ	sundesmō	bind together
4	hope	ἐλπίδι	elpidi	trust, confidence, guarantee security

5 One baptism (one way of being saved) the same act for all. Put Christ on by this ordinance.

6 One God, not a separate one for each nation (over, thru, in, epi, dia, ev).

7	measure	μέτρον	metron	standard, extent, portion

8 captive (many believe that Christ emptied out paradise, transfering the OT saints to heaven with Him as He ascended. After His ascension, He gave gifts unto men).

9 Before ascending, Christ first had to descend.

10 All true believers have been given some gift for the Lord's glory, some of which were exercised during the infancy stage of the Church (1 Cor. 13:8-10).

12 perfecting	καταρτισμὸν	katartismon (katartizō)	to mend; repair, adjust thoroughly, to frame complete in character
ministry	διακονίας	diakonias	serve
13 stature	ἡλικίας	hēlikias	particular period of life, full age, yrs, of discretion
14 carried about	πλάνης	planēs	to wander, as our planets
cunning craftiness	πανουργίᾳ	panourgia	trick, clever (craftiness can be good also)
slight	κυβείᾳ	kubeia (beuō)	play at dice (sometimes cheating)
13 Measure of the stature of the fullness of Christ.			
till we all attain	καταντήσωμεν	katantēsōmen (katantaō)	come down to goal. The gnostics were disturbing them at this time.
14 tossed to and fro	κλυδωνιζόμενοι	kludōnizomenoi (kludōn)	agitated as by waves (Jas. 1:6)
carried about with every wind	περιφερόμενοι	peripheromenoi	to whirl around as a hurricane or tornado

- Gifts are serving ministries: 1 Cor. 12:3-21, Eph. 4:1-16.
- Unity of the Spirit is the oneness of the faith in Christ (3).
- A worthy walk is a walk of love (2).
- Unity of the faith, perfect man, stature of the fullness of Christ, (each of these expresses the stability of the saint against the strong winds of false doctrine) (13, 14).
- Christians should grow up sometimes (14).
- Childish Christians misunderstand the doctrines of Christ (14).
- We all must be on guard against satanic perversion and deception (14).
- Young boys rejoice in gaining the height of a man; so should we in gaining the full measure of Christ (7, 13, 16).

New Life in the Home

EPH 5:21-6:4

Introduction:

New life in Christ begins in the home. A house can never be a home unless there is a loving family there, which our Lord brings. Thank God for new life, which obligates each family member.

Paul had been writing about the warfare of the Spirit filled believer; which includes: speaking to ourselves, making melody in our hearts, and giving thanks to God (Eph. 5:19, 20) in our text. He continues with another action word (vs. 21).

Translation, transliteration, interpretation:

v.	English	Greek	Transliterated	Alternative meanings
21	submitting	ὑποτασσόμενοι	hupotassomenoi	subordinate, under influence, rank self under

Paul is addressing believers. He uses this term some 23 times in other places in the NT. Similar passages: Rom. 12:10 (preferring one another in honor), Phil. 2:3 (esteeming others better), 2 Pe. 5:5 (clothed with humility), 1 Cor. 15:28 (the son is subject to the father).

v.	English	Greek	Transliterated	Alternative meanings
23	head	κεφαλὴ	kephalē	top, superior, chief, principle
26	sanctify	ἁγίασῃ	hagiasē (hagiazō)	hallow, pure, righteous
	cleanse	καθαρίσας	katharisa	guiltless, virtuous, innocent, sincere
	washing	λουτρῷ	loutrō	cleanse from sin
	word	ῥήματι	rhēmati (rheō)	saying, speech, mandate, prophecy, doctrine
27	might present	παραστήσῃ	parastēsē	place beside at disposal, devote, dedicate
	spot	σπίλον	spilon (spilos)	stain, moral blot, contaminate
	wrinkle	ῥυτίδα	rhutida	

128

	blemish	ἄμωμος	amōmos	blameless
28	bodies	σώματα	sōmata (sōma)	material substance
29	hate	ἐμίσησεν	emisēsen (miseō)	detest, abhor, ill will
	nourish	ἐκτρέφει	ektrephei	promote health and strength, bring up
	cherish	θάλπει	thalpei (thalpō)	to nurse, foster, impart warmth
31	shall leave	καταλείψει	kataleipsei	
	shall be joined	προσκολληθήσεται	proskollēthēsetai (proskollaō)	join self to anyone, cleave closely to
33	reverence	φοβῆται	phobētai	honor, respect
6:1	obey	ὑπακούετε	hupakouete (hubakouō)	harken, listen, submit
	right	δίκαιον	dikaion	judicial, just
6:2	promise	ἐπαγγελία	epaggelia (epaggellō)	favour, declare blessing
6:3	provoke not	παροργίζετε	parorgizete (parorgizō)	irritate, anger, wrath
6:4	nurture	παιδεία	paideia	training up, correction, instruction, discipline
	admonition	νουθεσία	nouthesia	warning, put in mind

Lessons from the lesson:
- Family Christian submission should be natural, not having to be forced (21).
- A loving family makes a house a home; Christ gives it life (22, 25; 6:1).
- The husband's headship is comparative to Christ's with the Church (23).
- The Church is the Bride of Christ (25-27).
- The wife is expected to submit to her own husband; not someone else's (22, 24).
- Husbands are to give themselves to their wives; Christ is our pattern (25).
- Christ's aim is to make the Church Holy with His Word (26).
- The Lord plans to present the Church, His Bride, to Himself after He cleans it up (27).
- The family is to operate in the fear of the Lord (as unto the Lord, 21, 22, 24, 25; 6:1, 4).
- The husband is the wife's saviour or protector or deliverer and defender (23).
- The husband should be worthy of the wife's submission (22, 23, 25, 28).

- One plus one equals one. The husband's love plus the wife's being joined, equals one flesh (31).
- Subordination must be met by love (25).
- The spoken Word of God cleanses. Spots and wrinkles hinder (27).
- Children can also provoke parents to wrath as well as the opposite (4).

Theology:

21	Submission, fear, God.
22	Lord, wives, husbands.
23	Head, Christ, Church, saviour, body.
25	Love, gift.
26	sanctify, cleanse, washing, Word.
27	Present, glorious, spot, wrinkle, Holy, blemish.
29	Hate, nourish, cherish.
30	Members, body, flesh, bones.
32	Mystery.
31	Father, mother, join.
33	Reverence.
6:1	Obedience, children, parenthood, just.
6:2	Honor, commandment, promise.
6:3	Life, earth.
6:4	Provocation, wrath, nurture, admonition.

Equipped for Life

EPH. 6:10-18

Introduction:

Both Jesus and the apostle Paul used many figures of speech; primarily metaphors. Both used metaphors of growth, planting, investment, and building. Paul also used metaphors of a race and boxing. Here it's one of spiritual warfare.

Translation, transliteration, interpretation:

v.	English	Greek	Transliterated	Alternative meanings
10	finally	τοῦ λοιποῦ	tou loipou	in respect of the rest, as for the rest
	be strong	ἐνδυναμοῦθε	endunamouthe	to empower, be empowered
	power	κράτει	kratei	might (see Acts 13:17)
	strong	ἰσχύος	ischuos	robust, might, power
11	whole armour	πανοπλίαν	panoplian	(panoply), suit of armour

Here Paul is not speaking particularly of completion as much as of God, for God's armour is complete if we put it on. If He spoke of completion, he obviously left off some things. Paul definitely was familiar with Roman armour, being chained to soldiers many times.

	English	Greek	Transliterated	Alternative meanings
	wiles	μεθοδείας	methodeias	artifices, scheme, craft, trickery, cunning
12	wrestle	πάλη	pallē	throw or swing, a contest of throwing or holding one down
	principalities	ἀρχας	archas	headship, priority
	powers	ἐξουσίας	exousias (exesti)	ability, authority, energy, dominion
	rulers	κοσμοκράτορας	kosmokratoras	world rulers, spiritually wicked hosts
	darkness	σκότοῦς	skotous	(rulers of this darkness)

wickedness	πονηρίας	ponērias	depravity (Matt. 22:18; 1 Cor. 5:8)
high places	ἐπουρανίοις	epouraniois	heavenly places
13 take up	ἀναλάβετε	analabete (analabōn)	picking up
withstand	ἀντιστῆναι	antistēnai (anthistēmi)	to stand face to face against
having done all	κατεργασάμενοι	katergasamenoi	having worked out, after the wrestling is over, to stand as victor
stand	στῆναι	stēnai	take your stand, in view of arguments made
14 loins	ὀσφὺν	osphun, (osphus)	
girt about	περιζωσάμενοι	perizōsamenoi	band around with a girdle, in preparation for bodily motion
breastplate	θώρακα	thōraka	breast
15 feet shod	ὑποδησάμενοι	hupodēsamenoi	bind under (sandals, Mk. 6:9, Acts 12:8)
peace	εἰρήνης	eirēnēs	
16 shield	θυρεὸν	thureon (thura)	as a large stone against a door
quench	σβέσαι (σβέννυμι)	sbesai (sbennumi)	to extinguish
fiery	πεπυρωμένα	pepurōmena	missile set on fire to burn enemy's clothes, etc
17 helmet	περικεφαλαίαν	perikephalain (kephalē)	head
sword	μάχαιραν	machairan	weapon (given by the Holy Spirit to wield)

The Word of God is sharper than a two-edged sword

18 praying	προσευχῆς	proseuchēs	
supplication	δεήσει	deēsei	spiritual embrace
watching	ἀγρυπνοῦντες	agrupnountes (agrupneō)	awake, vigilant
perseverance	προσκαρτερήσει	prostcarterēsei (proskartereō)	persist in adherence, attend constantly

all saints	πάντων τῶν ἁγίων	pantōn tōn hagiōn	hallowed, Holy, moral, righteous

Lessons from the lesson:
- We often fail because we either over estimate ourselves or underestimate Satan, or we don't claim God at all (10).
- The weapons of our warfare are not carnal, but mighty (2 Cor. 10:4).
- If God's power raised Jesus from the physically dead, and saints from the spiritually dead, He certainly can deliver us in our warfare (10).
- Satan's wiles are no match for God's armour (11).
- The world is watching parts of our wrestling match (12).
- Satan does his best work in the dark; with deceit and subtlety (12).
- 'High places' does not always infer high standards (12).
- Jesus has already won the battle at Calvary; that's where He spoiled all principalities and powers, making a shew of them openly, triumphing over them (Col. 2:15), leading captivity captive.
- Paul thought far less of the Roman Soldiers then Divine warriors (11).
- Christians are on the offensive as well the defensive (18).
- Stand here, doesn't mean only stand up, but, take a stand (13, 14).
- The darts of the wicked are fiery (16).
- Christians must-be prepared, knowing what we are up against, by trusting in the living God.
- Our prayers must include supplication (18).
- For a parallel passage see Isaiah 59:17, also Ps. 57:4 and 64:3.
- Satan trembles when he sees the weakest saint on his knees (18).

Theology:

10   Brethren, strength, Lordship, power, might.
11   Armour, God, wiles, devil.
12   Wrestle, blood, flesh, principalities, rulers, darkness, world, spiritual wickedness, high places.
13   Withstand evil.
14   Truth, breastplate, righteousness.
15   Gospel, peace.
16   Shield, faith, quench, fiery darts.
17   Helmet, salvation, sword, Spirit, Word of God.
18   Prayer, supplication, watchfulness, perseverance, saints.

Mutual Support

PHIL. 3:17-4:9

Introduction:

This letter was written by Paul, to the Church which he founded on his second missionary journey. Paul had met Lydia, a business woman, worshiping by the riverside with some of the other women of the city. This epistle was written from the prison in Rome. Paul, no doubt was remembering the charter members of the Church there; the jailer, his family, the demon possessed girl, the prisoners who heard Paul and Silas sing and pray, Lydia and her prayerful friends.

The city of Philippi was named after Philip of Macedon, father of Alexander the Great.

There probably were not enough Jews there to justify a Synagogue there, which explains the group of women worshipping down by the river.

Paul's writing to them was both circumstantial and instructional (and to a degree, doctrinal). He speaks of Christ's self emptying (ekenosen), His humility, and His exaltation. The enemies of the Cross of which he speaks, were Judaizers and Epicureans.

Translation, transliteration, interpretation:

v.	English	Greek	Transliterated	Alternative meanings
17	ensample	συμμιμηταί	summimētai	vie with each other, identify with examples, be joint imitators
18	enemies	ἐχθροὺς	exthrous	hostile, hated, disfavour
19	belly	κοιλία	koilia	sensuality (food, drink, sex)
20	conversation	πολίτευμα	politeuma	commonwealth, citizenship
21	vile	ταπεινώσεως	tapeinōseōs	depressed, humiliated, poor
	fashioned	σύμμορφον	summorphon	conformed
	working	ἐνέργειαν	energeian (energes)	energetic, effectual
	subdue	ὑποτάξαι	hupotaxai (hupotassō)	arrange, place, subordinate, bring under influence

4:1	longed for	ἐπιπόθητοι	epipothētoi	have affection for, desire earnestly, have strong bent
	joy	χαρὰ	chara	gladness
	crown	στέφανός	stephanos	victor's reward, prize, ornament
	stand fast	στήκετε	stēkete (histēmi)	endure, establish
4:3	yoke fellow	σύζυγε	suzuge	yoke together, conjoin, unite
	fellow labourers	συνεργῶν	sunergōn	associate, to assist
4:4	rejoice	χαίρετε	chairete	go on rejoicing
4:5	moderation	ἐπιεικὲς	epieikes (eikos)	sweet reasonableness, your gentleness
4:6	careful	μεριμνᾶτε	merimnate	stop being anxious
4:7	passeth understanding	ὑπερέχουσα	huperechousa	surpasses
	shall keep	φρουρήσει	phrourēsei	shall guard

Lessons from the lesson:
- We should not invite others to follow us if we are not following Christ (17).
- The lives of the saints should be exemplary (17).
- The walk of the enemies of Christ are dangerous steps (18).
- The belly calls for a selfish appetite (19).
- If our citizenship is in heaven, then we are pilgrims on earth (20).
- Our bodies are being fashioned to conform to the body of Christ (21).
- In times like these we must stand fast; not being blown about with every wind of doctrine (4).
- We should not take sides in disagreements of others but seek to arbitrate (4:2).
- Friction in the Church does not send a good message to the world (4:2).
- The Book of Life has the names of all of the righteous (4:3).
- There can be no real rejoicing apart from Christ (4:4).
- Jesus broke down the wall of separation (Judaism) which brought guilt, and death; the Jews during that time were trying to rebuild it (Eph. 2:14, 16).
- Worry is evidence of weak faith (6, Matt. 6:25-34).
- God will guard us if we trust in Him (4:7).
- When our minds are renewed we begin to think the right thoughts (4:8).

A Good Example

Introduction:

Timothy was Paul's son in the ministry. He was very faithful and Paul wanted him to be strong. Paul could see signs of apostasy approaching; as Peter (2 Pe.), John (2 & 3), and Jude. This is his second letter to Timothy; written shortly before his martyrdom.

Translation, Transliteration, interpretation:

v.	English	Greek	Transliterated	Alternative meanings
2:1	strong	ἐνδυναμοῦ	endunamou	empower, invigorate, be strengthened, put forth energy

Grace is the source of strength.

v.	English	Greek	Transliterated	Alternative meanings
2:2	commit	παράθου	parathou (paratithēmi)	to deposit
2:3	endure hardness	συγκακοπάθησον	sugkakopathēson	suffer evil, hold self back from
4:1	quick	ζῶντας	zōntas	living

Both they that have done good, and they that have done evil (Jn. 5:28, 29).

v.	English	Greek	Transliterated	Alternative meanings
	appearing	ἐπιφάνειαν	epiphaneian	manifest, display, be revealed
4:2	instant	ἐπίστηθι	epistēthi	urgent, take a stand, stand up to
	in season	εὐκαίρως	eukairōs	convenient time, opportunity, occasion

There are all kinds of seasons. Difficult seasons were on the way (3:1).

v.	English	Greek	Transliterated	Alternative meanings
	reprove	ἔλεγξον	elegxon	chide, blame, convict
	rebuke	ἐπιτίμησον	epitimēsan	reprimand, assess penalty
	exhort	παρακάλεσον	parakaleson	encourage
	longsuffering	μακροθυμία	makrothumia	patience
4:3	sound	ὑγιαινούσης	hugiainousēs (ugies)	wholesome, hale, sound in health or doctrine

136

	heap	ἐπισωρεύσουσιν (episoreuo)	episōreusousin	accumulate, produce in abundance, pile up
	itching	κνηθόμενοι (knaō)	knēthomenoi	to scratch, ακοην, *akoēn*, tickle, see Isaiah 30:10
4:4	fables	μύθους	muthous	a tale, lowest of figures of speech, earthly figure

The reaction to Stephen's preaching is a good example of turning ears away from the truth.

	turn away	ἐκτραπήσονται	ektrapēsontai	turn aside

Today's turning aside is to humanism and the so called "new thought".

4:5	full proof	πληροφόρησον	plērophorēson	fully carry out
	afflictions	κακοπάθησον	kakopathēson	evil (see vs. 3)

Lessons from the lesson:

- Regarding 4:4, Paul had referred to Timothy some of those who had turned away (1:15-18), Phygellus and Hermogenes; also 4:10 Demas, Crescens, and another Titus.
- God's grace not only saves us but it also sustains us (2:1) 2 Cor. 12:9.
- All Christians should be prepared for approaching persecution (3:12).
- If we suffer with Christ, we shall also reign with Him (2:12).
- The gospel must not be entrusted to just anyone; but faithful men (2:2).
- Todays teachers of the gospel must begin seeking men to replace us (2:2).
- The Church needs more teachers; we must pray that God would send more labourers in the vineyard.
- Paul uses many figures in describing the Christian worker; farmer 1 Cor. 3:6-9, builder. 1 Cor. 3:10 runner 9:24, boxer Eph. 6:13-17, Phil. 2:25, soldier (3).
- All persons are accountable to God, the Judge (4:1).
- Nothing can replace preaching the gospel (4:2).
- Good preaching (as we call it) should contain reproof, rebuking, and exhortation (4:2, 2:24, 25, Heb. 3:13).
- A faith worth having is worth passing on (2:3).
- Liberal theology is tickling many ears today (4:3).
- It is very easy to become discouraged (4:5).
- It is essential that we keep our eyes open (4:5).

Christ as God's Son

HEB. 1:1-4, 8-12

Introduction:

It appears evident that it wasn't Barnabus, Luke or Apollos that authored this Spirit filled epistle, but Paul; being called his 14th epistle. Let us confer with Peter (2 Peter 3:15, 16). Also, we may refer to Paul's salutations and benedictions; (2 Thess. 3:17, Heb. 13:23, 24).

The lesson is about Christ, the anointed, authorized, appointed Son of God. We will see that He is the supreme Revelation of God's identity; exceeding nature and Scripture (Luke 24:27).

Translation, transliteration, interpretation:

v.	English	Greek	Transliterated	Alternative meanings
1	sundry	πολυμερῶς	polumerōs	many portions
	divers	πολυτρόπως	polutropōs	many parts
	manners			
	God spoke	λαλήσας	lalēsas	

By signs, in voice, dreams, visions, etc.

To Adam (Gen. 3:15, 16), Noah (Gen. 6:13, 14), to Abraham (Gen. 12:1), to Isaiah, Jacob, Moses, David, Isaiah, Micah, etc. God also spake thru dispensations (Gal. 3:23-26, 4:4, 5).

v.	English	Greek	Transliterated	Alternative meanings
2	last	ἐσχάτου	eschatou	

See Acts 1:7, Luke 24:27, 44. There is no new revelation, beyond Christ (1 Pe. 3:22, 2 Pe. 1:21).

Christ is greater than Jonas (Lk. 11:32).

Christ is greater than Solomon (Matt. 12:42, Lk. 11:31).

Christ is greater than the Temple (Matt. 12:6).

English	Greek	Transliterated	Alternative meanings
appointed	ἔθηκεν	ethēken (tithēmi)	commit, assign
heir	κληρονόμον	klēronomon	a possessor (Gal. 4:1, 1 Pe. 1:20)

To give proof, show purpose (Jn. 8:35), show our right of adoption (Jn. 8:36, Rom. 8:17) by the determinate council, in form of a servant (Phil. 2:7-9, Heb. 5:5).

Made worlds (Jn. 1:3, Col. 1:16, 17).

3 brightness ἀπαυγασμα hapaugazma reflected brightness, effulgence

Brightness cannot be separated from the sun.

Brightness is of the same nature as the sun.

Brightness is never apart from the sun.

express image	χαρακτὴρ	charaktēr (charassō)	to cut, scratch, mark: Acts 17:29, Rev. 13:16
person	ὑποστάσεως	hupostaseōs	substance
upholding	φέρων	pherōn	to bear, carry, conduct, bring forth
word	ῥήματι	rhēmati (rheō)	to speak, mandate, command, predict, prophesy

3 purged καθαρισμὸν katharismon cleanse, (Matt. 8:3, Heb. 9:14, 28)

majesty μεγαλωσύνης megalōsunēs (megas) greatness, ascribed majesty

4 better κρείττων kreittōn

more excellent διαφορώτερον diaphorōteron superior to prophets 1:2, superior to angels 1:4, 2:18

Ps. 97:7: 'Let all angels worship Him.' Deut. 32:43, Luke 2:13, Ps. 89:28.

8 O God (Ps. 45:6, 7, Is. 9:6, 7, 11:1-5)

sceptre ῥάβδος rhabdos walking stick, staff, (Heb. 11:21)

9 anointed ἔχρισέν echrisen (ohriō) (Christos)

fellows μετόχους metochous (metechō) partners, sharers

10 hast laid foundation ἐθεμελίωσας ethemeliōsas (themelloō) foundation: Ps. 102:23-25, Col. 1:23

11 See Isaiah 50:9, Heb. 13:8.

12 See 2nd Pe. 3:7, 10.

There is a difference between Creation and the Creator (pantheism, materialism)

Application:
- The Bible is of Divine authority (1).
- God is in Christ (1).
- Jesus is God's final message to the world (1).
- The best things are reserved for the last times (1).
- Indeed, God has spoken (1).

- God exalted Christ; so should we (4).
- If we love rightousness we will hate evil (9).
- We cannot really appreciate Creation without recognizing its Creator (10).

Theology:

1) God, time, dispensation, revelation, figures, prophecy, forefathers.
2) Eschatology, Sonship, Divine purpose, Creation.
3) Glory, image, person of God, sovereignty, Word of God, omnipotence, sin, cleansing, Authority, majesty
4) Superiority.
8) Throne, eternity, sceptre, righteousness, Kingdom.
9) Love, iniquity, anointment.
10) Earth, beginning, heaven, works.
11, 12) Finiteness, immutability, time, eternity, death.

Christ as Our Redeemer

HEB. 9:11-18; 10:12-14, 17-18

Introduction:

The word in our subject, redeem, is the translation of the Greek word lutron, which means 'a ransom paid to dismiss.' This ransom was not paid to Satan for the dismissal of sinful man, as some have projected; but this ransom was paid as a propitiation to the Holy God, who had been offended by the sins of man; for his forgiveness, acceptance, and favour.

Translation, transliteration, interpretation:

v.	English	Greek	Transliterated	Alternative meanings
11	high priest	ἀρχιερεὺς	archiereus	

Christ also came as prophet (Deut. 18:15, 18) and king (Matt. 2:2).

His work was expiatory, reconciling, and meditorial (8:3, 1 Tim. 2:5, 6).

Christ being come (Ps. 40:7).

	English	Greek	Transliterated	Alternative meanings
	good things	ἀγαθῶν	agathōn	profitable, virtuous, benevolent
	to come	μελλοντων	mellontōn (mellō)	about to, that are come

The good things which have come are of grace and glory.

	English	Greek	Transliterated	Alternative meanings
	more perfect	τελειοτέρας	teleioteras (telos)	developed, complete, fully accomplished (Heb. 10:5, 20, 8:2, Jn. 1:14)
	not made by hand	οὐ χειροποιῆτου	ou cheiropoiētou	

The tabernacle was made by hand (Ex. 36:1-8, Dan. 2:45).

	English	Greek	Transliterated	Alternative meanings
	this building	κτίσεως	ktiseōs (ktizō)	create, call into being
12	His own	ἰδίου	idiou	one's own (Christ is the antitype)
	entered	εἰσῆλθεν	eisēlthen,	enter into, take possession (9:8, 24, Ps. 20:6)
	once	ἐφάπαξ	ephapax	once for all (Rom. 6:10)
	having obtained	εὑράμενος	heuramenos (euraiskō)	having found

13	sanctify	ἁγιάζει	hagiazei (hagaios)	hallowed, pure, righteous
	purify	καθαρότητα	katharotēta	guileless, innocent, sincere, clean, unfeigned
14	how much more	πόσῳ μᾶλλον	posō mallon	in preference, to greater extent, higher
	offered	προσήνεγκεν	prosēnegken	
	Himself	ἑαυτὸν	heauton	
	degree without spot	ἄμωμον	amōmon	blameless
	purge	καθαριεῖ	kathariei	clean from guilt, purify. See Jn. 8:36; Gal. 3:13
	conscience	συνείδησιν	suneidēsin (sunoida)	moral judgement
15	mediator	μεσίτης	mesitēs	middle, between, midst
	new	καινῆς	kainēs	
	testament	διαθήκης	diathēkēs	compact, agreement

This term diatheke is used in the New Testiament some 33 times; translated in the A.V. Covenant 20 times; it is also translated bequeathal or free gift; 4 times Lord's Supper.

	redemption	ἀπολύτρωσιν	apolutrōsin	a ransom paid for a dismissal (Rom. 4:25; Gal 1:4)
	transgressions	παραβάσεων	parabaseōn (parabainō)	deviate, violate, stepping by the side
	promise	ἐπαγγελίαν	epaggelian,	declare, announce, profess
16	testator	διαθεμένου	diathemenou	make a disposition, assign
	dedicated		eggkainazo	consecrate, inaugurated
10:12	sat down	ἐκάθισεν	ekathizev	place, stay, be seated
10:13	expecting	ἐκδεχόμενος	ekdechomenos	looking for, awaiting
10:14	He has perfected	τετελείωκεν	teteleiōken	
10:17	iniquities	ἀνομιῶν	anomiōn, (onomos)	without law, lawlessness

Application:
- It was to God that Jesus offered Himself a propitiation for sin (14).
- Good things have come and are coming by Christ (11).

- Once is enough (12, 7:27).
- Christ renders us propitious to God (14).
- We are purged to serve (14).
- Christ is better, greater, more perfect (9, 14).
- Jesus is Christ: *anointed*, Ps. 2:2, Acts 4:26; *the Christ*, Jn. 20:31; *that Christ*, Jn. 6:69; *very Christ*, Acts 9:22; *the Lord's Christ*, Lk. 2:26; *Christ of God*, Lk. 9:20.

Christ superior to Aaron:

11	He officiated in a more excellent tabernacle.
11, 14	He offered a superior sacrifice.
12	He entered a more glorious sanctuary.
12	He secured a more efficacious redemption.
14	He was moved by a more excellent Spirit.
14	He rendered a better cleansing.
14	He enabled us to offer a nobler service.

- The effect of Christ's atonement was retrospective (looking back) and prospective (present & future 1 Jn. 1:7; 1 Pe. 1:19-20) Rom. 3:25.
- External works cannot bring internal cleansing (13, 14).

Theology:

11	Christ, priesthood, tabernacle, perfection, Creation.
12	Sacrifice, blood, Holy place, eternity, redemption.
13	Sanctification, purification, humanity.
14	Holy spirit, offering, propitiation, conscience, living God.
15	Mediation, new Covenant, death, redemption, expiation, transgression, old Covenant promise, inheritance.
16	Will of Christ.
18	Dedication.
10:12	Sin, anthropomorphism.
10:13	Enemy, sovereignty of Christ.
10:17	Iniquity, forgiveness.
10:18	Remission.

Lessons from the lesson:

- God has designed an Eternal Inheritance unto certain persons.
- The way in which a title or right is conveyed is by promise.

- The persons unto whom this inheritance is designed are the Called.
- The obstacle standing in the way of their enjoyment of this inheritance was their transgressions.
- This obstacle might be removed and inheritance enjoyed. God made a New Cov. Because none of the sacrifices of the 1st Cov. could expiate away sin.
- The ground of the efficacy of the New Cov. to this end was that it had a mediator––a great High Priest.
- The means whereby the mediator of the New Cov. did expiate the sin against the 1st Cov. was by death. Seeing that this New Cov. being also a new Testament, required the death of a testator.
- The death of this mediator has taken away sins by the redemption of transgressions. Thus the promise is sure unto all the seed.

Christ as Eternal God

HEB. 13:1-16

Introduction:

In this series of lessons, we have studied about Christ: as God's Son; as intercessor; as redeemer; and as leader. Today we will see that He is the eternal changeless God who is ever-present with His people.

Translation, transliteration, interpretation:

v.	English	Greek	Transliterated	Alternative meanings
1	continue	μενέτω	menetō	let abide

The Christians in this epistle had brotherly love already, but there was danger of it disappearing because of continuing pressure from without.

They are reminded that God hasn't forgotten their faithfulness (6:10).

The fruit of the Spirit is love (Gal. 5:22. See 1 Jn. 5:1; 2 Pe. 1:7; Acts 16:33; Jn. 13:35).

v.	English	Greek	Transliterated	Alternative meanings
2	entertained	ξενίσαντες	xenisantes	to be hospitable to a guest

The reference here is to Abraham and Sarah entertaining two unexpected and unrecognized angels.

v.	English	Greek	Transliterated	Alternative meanings
3	bonds	δεσμίων	desmiōn	prisoners (10:34)
	adversity	κακουχουμένων	kakouchoumenōn	evil treatment
4	in all	ἐν πᾶσιν	en pasin	in every way
	undefiled	ἀμίαντος	amiantos	unsoiled, unstained, chaste
5	without love of money	ἀφιλάργυρος	aphilarguros	genuine, liberal
	content	ἀρκούμενοι	arkoumenoi	suffice, satisfied
6	helper	βοηθός	boēthos	to help. Reference Ps. 118:61; see also Matt. 9:2; 2 Cor. 5:6, 8.
8	same	αυτὸς	autos	
9	doctrines	διδαχαῖς	didachais (didaktos)	teachings
	various	ποικίλαις	poikilais	diverse, manifold

		Greek	Transliteration	Meaning
	established	βεβαιῶσθαι	bebaiusthai	confirmed
	occupied	περιπατοῦντες	peripatountes	walked
11	are burned	κατακαίεται	katakaietai	to burn up, consume
	without	ἔξω	exo	outside
12	blood	αἵματος	haimatos	
	suffered	ἔπαθεν	epathen pascho	endure evil, be affected by
13	go forth	ἐξερχώμεθα	exerchōmetha	proceed, emanate, depart
16	is well pleased	εὐαρεστεῖται	euaresteitai	acceptable, take pleasure

Lessons from the lesson:
- We Christians are brothers, with one father, and one elder brother who is not ashamed to call us brethren (2:11, Rom. 8:29).
- We are to continue in God's New Commandment (Jn. 13:34).
- Brotherly love has some hindrances: self love; and worldly love (see 1 Cor 13).
- Brotherly love is: φιλαδελφια, philadelphia.
- A needful word,
- An humbling word,
- A solemn word,
- A gracious word,
- A comprehensive word.
- It is always in order for Christians to show love to strangers (2).
- Brotherly love is manifested in hospitality and remembering the bonds of others thru prayer and deeds of kindness (vs. 2; Eph. 6:18-20; Col. 4:18).
- Brotherly love and hospitality take risks; but the blessings out weigh the risks (2).
- Christians are not only to sympathize with others, but to empathize with them (3, 1 Cor. 12:26).
- We are sometimes so taken up with our own ills that we forget the ills of others (3).
- Our society may be lenient to adulterers, but God is not (4).
- God may forgive sexual sin, but the Church should never condone it (4).
- Christians are to cultivate contentment rather than greed (5).
- We need not vex ourselves because of daily need; God has promised His companionship (Gen. 28:15 Deut. 31:6, 8; Josh. 1:5).
- God not only is our provider but He is our protector (6).
- We should remember the fruit of our exemplars (Heb. 11).
- We should avoid useless teaching (9, Eph. 4:14).
- We are to partake of the reproach with Christ, outside the camp (13).

- Praise and thanksgiving are well pleasing to God (15, 16).
- Blest be the tie that binds our hearts in Christian love.
- The fellowship of kindred minds is like to that above
- We share our mutual woes, our mutual burdens bear.
- And often for each other flows the sympathizing tear.

Doers of the Word

JAS. 1:17-27

Introduction:

There is an old saying that was very prominent in the past, "actions speak louder than words." This saying is very prominent in the text. James is addressing Jewish Christians who were exemplifying unChristianlike conduct in their speech and in their doctrine. Let us take note.

Translation, transliteration, interpretation:

v.	English	Greek	Transliterated	Alternative meanings
17	gift	δόσις	dosis (didōmi)	to give, act of giving
		δώρημα	dōrēma (dorsō, doron)	a gift, benefaction
	variableness	παραλλαγὴ	parallagē (parallassō)	alternate, variation
	shadow	ἀποσκίασμα	aposkiasma	turning of a shadow
	turning	τροπῆς	tropēs (trepō)	to turn
18	begat	ἀπεκύνσεν	apechunsen (apokueō)	

This is referring to our regeneration. Word of truth refers to the gospel which is marked by truth.

	first fruits	ἀπαρχήν	aparchēn (aparchomai)	some first fruits
19	swift	ταχὺς	taxus	
	slow	βραδὺς	bradus	

Against boiling rage and violent disputatious speech (3:1-12).

20	righteousness	δικαιοσύνην	dikaiosunēn	
	worketh not	ἐργάζεται	ergazetai	works not out
21	lay apart	ἀποθέμενοι	apothemenoi (apotithēmi)	removing clothing
	filthiness	ῥυπαρίαν	rhuparian	dirty (2:2)
	superfluity	περισσείαν	perisseian	abundant, overflowing

148

	wickedness	κακίας	kakias	
	naughtiness	πραΰτητι	prautēti	
	engrafted	ἔμφυτον	emphuton	to implant, ingrown
22	hearers	ἀκροατὴς	akroatēs	

This is self delusion, miscalculation.

23	beholding	κατανοοῦντι	katanoounti	take note of, put the mind on, considering
	natural	γενέσεως	geneseōs	to come into existence
	glass	ἐσόπτρῳ	esoptrō	mirror
25	continueth	παραμείνας	paramemeinas	stay beside remain, persevere
	liberty	ἐλευθερίας	eleutherias	freedom, exempt, unrestricted
26	seem	δοκεῖ	dokei	think, imaging, suppose, presume
	bridleth	χαλιναγωγῶν	chalinagōgōn (chalinos)	put a bridle on one's mouth,
	not deceive	ἀπατῶν	apatōn	play a trick on one's self
	vain	μάταιος	mataios	ineffective, fruitless, unprofitable
27	unspotted	ασπιλους	aspilon (spilos)	spot (alt)
	pure	καθαρὰ	kathara	clean
	undefiled	ἀμιαντὸν	amianton	to defile not

Lessons from the lesson:

- All of God's gifts are good and perfect, and changeless (17).
- God was not forced to bring us into existence (18).
- We should listen more and speak less (19).
- The wrath of man and the Holy wrath of God are quite different (20).
- Worldly anger is not the best way to please God (20).
- Christians should separate themselves from certain actions (21).
- We should watch out for overactive tongues (19) there are some who talk too much.
- Wrath is a bad attitude (20).
- Everyone who disagrees with you is not your enemy (20).
- Wrath contradicts the very righteousness that we claim to be defending (20).
- Hearing God's Word is not enough (23).
- God's Word is a mirror, revealing something in us that needs improving (23).
- When we look at ourselves in a mirror, often, we don't think anything needs to be changed (24).
- The world is full of spots, but we needn't get any on us (27).

Wise Speakers

JAS. 3:1-10, 13-18

Introduction:

Solomon said that death and life are in the power of the tongue (Prov. 18:21); Jeremiah said that the tongue is an arrow shot out (Jer. 9:8). Solomon also said (Prov. 21:23) whoso keepeth his tongue keepeth his soul from trouble. A lying tongue is one of the things that God hates (Pr. 6:7). Today's lesson is about the tongue. Let us see what James has to say about its dangers.

Translation, transliteration, interpretation:

v.	English	Greek	Transliterated	Alternative meanings
1	masters	διδάσκαλοι	didaskaloi (didaskō)	to teach, direct, admonish, doctrine

Stop becoming many teachers; teaching what you don't clearly understand (3:13). James issues a clear call for wise teachers, rather than foolish. Godly teachers are God called (1 Cor. 12:28, 14:26), considered as wise men (Jas. 3:13) and honorable (Eph. 4:11). James counted himself a teacher. Teachers are necessary in the Church, but a foolish incompetent one can do much harm.

	English	Greek	Transliterated	Alternative meanings
	greater	μεῖζον	meizon	heavier, more intense
	condemnation	κρίμα	krima	judgement, sentence from the judge
2	we offend	πταίομεν	ptaiomen	fail, stagger, stumble, err, transgress, false step
	bridle	χαλιναγωγῆσαι	chalinagōgēsai	control, guide with a bridle:

Titus 1:11, Paul told Titus that the mouths of some must be muzzled; ἐπιστομίζειν, *spistomizein*.

	English	Greek	Transliterated	Alternative meanings
3	obey	πείθεσθαι	peithesthai	
	we turn about	μετάγομεν	metagomen (metagō)	to guide, change direction
4	ships	πλοῖα	ploia (pleō)	sail

Paul's ship to malta carried as many as 276 persons (Acts 27:37).

driven	ἐλαυνόμενα	elaunomena (elauvō)	spur on, urge forward, rowing
fierce	σκληρῶν	sklērōn (skellō)	harsh, stiff, rough
turned about (see vs. 3			
helm	πηδαλίου	pēdaliou	blade, oar, rudder
governor	εὐθύνοντος	euthunontos (eunthunō, euthus)	He who steers, guide
listeth,	ὁρμὴ	hormē	impulse
5 member	μέλος	melos	limb, member of human body (1 Cor. 12:12)
boasteth great things	μεγάλα αὐχεῖ	megala auchei	vaunt, cause great stir, boast
great matter	ἡλίκον	hēliken	
a wood	ὕλην	hulēn	
kindleth	ἀνάπτει	anaptei	to light, set on fire
6 (world of) iniquity	(κόσμος τῆς) ἀδικίας	adikias (adikeō)	wrong, unjust, falsehood
defileth	σπιλοῦσα	spilousa (spilos)	spot, stain, moral blot
course	τροχὸν	trochon (trechō)	course of conduct, track, path, way
7 tame	δαμάζεται	damazetai (damazō)	restrain, subdue
8 unruly evil when set on fire of hell	ἀκατάστατον	akatastaton	commotion, disorder, ungodly
deadly poison	θανατηφόρου	thanatēphorou	(thanatos=death + phero=bear) death bringing
9 bless	εὐλογοῦμεν	eulogoumen	a good word
curse	καταρώμεθα	katarōmetha (katara)	a curse
similitude	ὁμοίωσιν	homoiōsin	resembling likeness
13 good conversation	ἀναστροφῆς	anastrophēs	walk, conduct, good life

Lessons from the lesson:

- In the lesson today look for metaphors of horse, ships, fire, animal, and serpent.
- Teaching God's Word is a solemn task and is not to be taken lightly (1, 2).
- Dont let your tongue master you (1).
- The sin of the tongue is the last to be conquered (2).
- One who controls the tongue is close to maturity (2).
- Some men follow their mouths which often gets them in trouble (6).
- The tongue can start a fire without matches (6) it strikes too.
- The fire of the tongue is from Gehenna, hell (6).
- Human inability doesn't mean Divine inability (8).
- One tongue is bad enough; but to be double tongued is twice as bad (9, 10); Prov. 6:24, Ps. 5:9, Prov 10:7.
- An offensive tongue leaves a bitter taste (14); Heb. 12:14; Eph. 4:31.
- Wisdom is proven by good conduct (13).
- Word damage remains even after forgiveness has been bestowed (14).
- Words, good or bad, about people, reflect our relationship with God (9, 10).
- There are 2 kinds of wisdom; 1 from above, and 1 from below (15, 17).
- Words are powerful, and carry a powerful responsibility (13).
- Sow peace and reap righteous fruit (18).
- All saints should at least be able to teach others about salvation (Heb. 5:12; 1 Peter 3:15).

Prayerful Community

JAS. 5:13-18

Introduction:

Prayer is communicating with the Creator; even without words and sound we can pray. Prayer is not only asking but receiving. Prayer is an attitude, an expression, a condition, an atmosphere, and a spectrum in which all men should engage. It is a tool, a weapon, and a gift from God. In the lesson today, James is enjoining his hearers to make use of this obligatory emotion.

Translation, transliteration, interpretation:

v.	English	Greek	Transliterated	Alternative meanings
13	afflicted	κακοταθεῖ	kakopathei	suffering evil
	pray	προσευχέσθω	proseuchesthō	keep on praying, continue praying
	sing	ψαλλέτω	psalletō (psallō)	keep on making music
14	sick	ἀσθενεῖ	asthenei (astheeō)	weak, without strength
	call for	προσκαλεσάσθω	proskalesasthō	request, send for
	elder	πρεσβυτέρους	presbuterous	this same word is translated bishop, elder (Acts 20:12, 15:6, 22, 21:18, Phil. 1:1)
	anoint	ἀλείψαντες	aleipsantes (aleiphō)	to smear with oil (elaio)

Oil was then used medicinally, as a rubbing compound; it was also taken internally.

v.	English	Greek	Transliterated	Alternative meanings
15	sick	κάμνοντα	kamnonta	exhausted one, to be weary
	save	σώσει	sōsei	make well
	forgiven	ἀφεθήσεται	aphethēsetai (aphiēmi)	change of heart
16	confess	ἐξομολογεῖσθε	exomologeisthe (exomologeō)	

It is assumed that confession to God had already been made.

We must be careful to whom we confess, and what we confess.

v.	English	Greek	Transliterated	Alternative meanings
	faults	παραπτωματα	paraptōmata	offenses (alt)

effectual	ἐνεργουμένη	energoumenē (energeō)	when exercised
availeth much	πολὺ ἰσχύει	polu ischuei	much prevails
17 like passions	ὁμοιοπαθὴς	homoiopathēs	suffering the like with another
fervent	ζρο \rtts	zeontes (zaō)	vitality (Jn. 4:10, intense 1 Peter 1:3)
rain	βρέξαι	brexai	moisture
18 brought forth	ἐβλάστησεν	eblastēsen	caused to sprout
fruit	καρπὸν	karpon	

Lessons from the lesson:

- James is said to be the earliest of the New Testament writers, writing around. 45 A.D.
- James' writing is believed to have been before the Jerusalem council, also before the Gentiles were received in the congregation.
- Affliction is not the only means of sickness (13).
- Prayer has many occasions (13).
- God may not remove the suffering but He gives strength to endure it (13).
- Being merry is just as important in praising God as trials (13, Eph. 5:19, 20).
- God is both the source and the object of our praise (13).
- We should live in an atmosphere of prayer and be thankful for its spectrum (13).
- Paul and Silas sang while suffering (Acts 16:25).
- God uses our prayers as means by which He accomplishes His will (15).
- Love refuses to see faults (15, 1 Peter 4:8; Jas. 5:20).
- Some illnesses are due to sin (15).
- When a Christian brother or sister is sick, don't wait to be called on before praying for them.
- There are some who call on the elders unceasingly (14).
- Prayer without faith is vain (15).
- Confession of offenses lightens the load of sin and aides in our spiritual health (15).
- Prayer is effectual when it is operating (16).
- Prayer is both offensive and defensive (17, 18).
- Both the beginning and the end of a drought in Israel came through prayer (17, 18).
- Hatred stirs up strife; but love will hide transgressions (20, Prov. 10:12).

A Holy People

1 PE. 1:13-25

Introduction:

Holiness is God's basic attribute; it is fundamental in the life of His saints. Without holiness no one can have fellowship with the Lord. We know holiness in God in the form of righteousness and justice. Peter reminds us that the saints are a Holy Nation (1 Pe. 2:9). Holiness is reflected in the conduct of the saints. In today's lesson we will see that Jesus paid the price for our holiness, love is its sign, and the Word of God is its seed.

Translation, transliteration, interpretation:

v.	English	Greek	Transliterated	Alternative meanings
13	gird	ἀναζωσάμενοι	anazōsamenoi (zaō)	full, unflowing

This describes the action of gathering the loose robe.

| | loins | ὀσφύας | osphuas (osphus) | the part of the body where the girdle was worn |

The "loins of the mind" is a metaphor, meaning to think clearly and freely.

| | sober | νερομένην | neromenēn | vigilant, not intoxicated |
| | revelation | ἀποκαλύψει | apokalupsei (apokalupsō) | manifestation, appearance |

Here the apostle is speaking of the rapture, the coming of Christ for the saints.

14	fashioning	συσχηματιζόμενοι	suschēmatizomenoi (schēma)	the outward pattern (vs. inward change)
	inward lusts	ἐπιθυμίαις	epithumiais	desires (can be good or evil, here evil)
15	Holy	ἅγιοι	hagioi	separate, hallowed, morally pure
	conversation	ἀναστροφῇ	anastrophē	conduct, behavior

In Peter's epistles he uses this term 8 times: 1:15, 18, 2:12, 3:1, 3:16, 2 Pe. 2:7, 3:11.

17	sojourning	παροικίας	paraoikias (paroikeō)	to dwell beside in one's neighborhood
18	corruptible	φθαρτοῖς	phthartois (phtheirō)	spoil, ruin, morally depraved
	redeemed	ἐλυτρώθητε	elutrōthēte (lutroō, luō)	disengage, unfasten, unbind, untie,
	tradition	ἀναστροφῆς	anastrophēs (strephō)	turn back, returnloosen
19	without blemish	ἀμώμου	amōmou	blameless (see Isaiah 53:7)
	without spot	ἀσπίλου	aspilou	spotless, unblemished
20	last times	ἐσχάτου	eschatou	sfarthest, latest, last (this is the doctrine of eschatology)
	foreordained	προεγνωσμένου	proegnōsmenou	determine beforehand, acquainted
22	purified	ἡγνικότες	hegnikotes (hagnizō)	pure, chaste, modest, innocent
	unfeigned	ἀνυπόκριτον	anupokritov	real, sincere (Rom. 12:9)
	fervent	ἐκτενῶς	ekteinōs	intense, earnest
24,	see Isaiah 40:6-8, Jas. 1:11			
25				

Lessons from the lesson:

- The hope of the saints is to the end (13).
- We should be getting our minds together (13).
- Grace will be brought to the saints by Jesus in the resurrection (13).
- We are not to be conformed to this world as we used to (14).
- God's Word is our standard (15, 25).
- God is no respecter of persons (17).
- Our redemption was at a high cost (18).
- Our prior manner of life was vain, accomplishing nothing for the Lord (18).
- The love of the saints is to be mutual, sincere and intense (22).

- Love for others is not to be presumed but practiced (22).
- The Word of God is seed and sanctification is its growth; eternity is its end (23, 25).

Theology:
- Jesus Christ, hope, grace, eschatology, revelation.
- Lusts, obedience, ignorance, conformation.
- Calling, holiness, conduct.
- Scripture.
- Fatherhood of God, God the Judge, works of man.
- Redemption, corruption, conduct, tradition.
- Blood of Christ, lamb, spotlessness.
- Foreordination, Creation, apocalypse.
- Faith, resurrection, death, glory.
- Sanctification, Holy Spirit, soul, truth, love, brotherhood.
- Corruption, Word of God, life, eternity.
- Flesh, glory of man.
- Gospel.

A Chosen People

1 PE. 2:1-10

Introduction:

The lesson today is about the Bible doctrine of Election (see Exodus 19:6; Deut. 7:6, 14:2; Rev. 1:6, 5:10). God has a right to choose; and He does make choices of people for His purpose. In this lesson, He makes choice of a Holy Nation.

Translation, transliteration, interpretation:

v.	English	Greek	Transliterated	Alternative meanings
1	laying aside	ἀποθέμενοι	apothemenoi	put off clothing, putting away
	malice	κακίαν	kakian	to count worthless, depraved, wicked
	guile	δόλον	dolon	deceit, to catch with bait, a trap (skandalon, σκανδάλον)
	hypocrisies	ὑποκρίσεις	hupokriseis	antonyms: (real, sincere, unfeigned, not acting)
	envies	φθόνους	phthonous	jealousy, spite
	evil speakings	καταλαλιάς	katalalias	to defame, backbite (Rom. 1:30, 31; 1 Pe. 2:12)
	These are all impediments to growth.			
2	sincere	ἄδολον	adolon	no guile, genuine
	milk	γάλα	gala	
	newborn	βρέφη	brephē	infant
	desire	ἐπιποθήσατε	epipothēsate	long for, intense yearning
3	tasted (from persue)	ἐγεύσατε	egeusate (geuomai)	to excite the appetite
4	disallowed	ἀποδεδοκιμασμένον	apodedokimasmenon	to reject upon trial (Ps. 118:22, Matt. 2:42, Mk. 12:10, Lk. 20:17, Acts 4:11)
5	lively	ζῶντες	zōntes (zaō)	vitality, living, life
6	confounded	καταισχυνθῇ	kataischunthē	put to shame, frustrate, disgrace
7	precious	τιμὴ	timē	estimate of worth, value, honor

8	stumbling	προσκόμματος	proskommatos	to fall by accident because of an obstacle
	appointed	ἐτέθησαν	etethēsan (tithēmi)	to appoint, design, assign, to set (Is. 8:14)
9	chosen	ἐκλεκτόν	eklekton	an elect race of people (see Isaiah 43:20)
	royal	βασίλειον	basileion	regal authority, of a Kingdom, reign, dominion
	Holy	ἅγιον	hagion	
	peculiar	περιποίησιν	peripoiēsin	special for God's own possession
	marvellous	θαυμαστὸν	thaumaston	admiration, astonishment, wonder
10	not a people	οὐ λαὸς	ou laos	(not a nation of God)
	received mercy	ἠλεημένοι	eleēmenoi (eleeō, eleos)	compassion, kindness

Lessons from the lesson:

- All manner of sin must be laid aside in order to be a part of God's Holy Nation (2:1).
- Believers in Christ must become as growing infants in God's school of righteousness (2:2).
- All those who have experienced the Lord know without a doubt that He is gracious (2:3).
- If the world rejected Christ, surely the world will reject His followers (2:4).
- The Lord is spiritually constructing His Church, and His followers are living stones in it (2:!
- Each follower of the Lord is a priest (2:5).
- What a mistake, to reject the Chief Cornerstone of the building (2:4).
- If God accepts us, why fear? He is more than the world that is against us (2:5).
- God put His choice in writing (2:6).
- To all of the saints, Christ is precious (2:4, 6, 7).
- There are many who stumble over Christ, who is in their pathway (2:8).
- God has called the saints out of darkness into His astonishing, radiant light (2:9).
- God has a right to choose (2:9).
- God's people are peculiar, not to each other, but to the world (2:9).
- Man's plans cannot hinder God's purpose (7, 8).

2nd Edition

Alpha and Omega

REV. 22:12-21

Introduction:

The words in the text are the same as in vs. 7, Behold, I come quickly. These words have also been spoken in 3:11 and 22:20. Come quickly, taxus, means soon, speedily, shortly, suddenly, and with haste. This seems to be a warning to the wicked and the unprepared.

The subject Alpha αλφα and Omega ομεγα are Greek alphabets with which the Lord identifies Himself. This makes these alphabets in English grammar, called appositions, and personifications. This term is applied to God the Father (21:6) and to Christ the Son 22:13.

Speaking of alphabet, the Lord is also the Aleph αλεφ and the Tau ταυ of the Hebrew alphebet.

• •

Translation, Transliteration, Interpretation:

12) Reward, μισθος Misthos, that which is due (Heb. 11:6; Isaiah 40:10, 62:11; Rev. 11:18

13) Beginning, αρχη arche

End, τελος Telos

First, πρωτος Protos (1:17, 2:8)

Last, εσχατος Eschatos

* Since Christ is the author αρχηγος Archegos and finisher τελειωτης Teleiotes of all things He is qualified to be Judge of man's works (Vs. 12) (see Heb. 12:2)

14) In this verse the narrative changes from God to John.

A right, εξουσια exousia, authority, power over, (6:8, 13:7, 16:9, lk. 9:1
* These are said to have washed their robes in the blood of the lamb. This doesn't mean that their salvation is by their own merit Eph. 2:8, 9, but by God's work Jn. 6:29.

15) Without (outside) the Holy city are dogs κυνες kunes, not literal dogs but immoral and impure Deut. 23:18.

Sorcerers, φαρμακοι pharmakoi, drugs, spells, witchcraft (21:8; Matt. 8:12; Mk. 9:48

Idolaters, _____ eidololatres, worshipping and serving idols
* God has already declared Himself to be a jealous God (Ex. 20:5)

Making a lie (21:8) ποιων, poison, doing, practicing deceit, not practicing truth

A lie, ψευδος pseudos, a falsehood, deception 2 Cor. 2:12; Rom. 1:25; Eph. 4:25
* Satan is father of lying Jn. 8:44 his home is the place of lying.

16) Testify, μαρτυρησαι Maturesai, to witness, give evidence, confirmation

Offspring, γενος genos, birth, produce, growth Acts 17:28

Morning Star, φωσφορος phosphoros, and Num. 24:17; Lk. 1:78, Day star 2 Pet.1:19 ορθριζω orthrizo, early dawn, first streak of daybreak

17) here is a group of invitations:
Ερχεσθω erchestho

The Holy Spirit of prophecy and the Bride say come let him come (he that desires to meet Christ he that is thirsty _____dipsao, spiritually whosoever will o thelon (even if not eagerly thirsting yet
* Here is a welcome to a thirst quenching party

18) Add, επιθησαι Epithesai (epitithemi), to attach, impose, place upon

19) Take away, αφαιρη Aphaire, remove, cut off, take off

his part, μερος meros, division, portion, piece, fragment

There are three testimonies in the lesson:
One by the Angel sent from God (1:1)
One from the Lord Himself (18)
Another by the Lord (20)

20) Amen, αμην amen, affirmation, assent, truth, verily, certainly, so be it, I agree

• •

Practical lessons:
* The Jesus of history is the Christ of theology. (16) (13)
* There will be no opportunity for change when Christ's coming occurs. (11)
* When Christ arrives, it will be sudden and unexpected to the wicked. (12)
* The wicked will be rewarded also. (12)
* Since time is in God He controls its beginning and ending. (1:17, 2:8, 21:6, 22:13)
* The water of life is free. (21:6, 22:17)
* The saints have free access to the New Jerusalem and all of its contents. (21:12, 25, 22:2)
* Outside of the City is immorality. Deut. 23:18; Matt. 7:6; Rev. 20:11-15
* Christ is heir to David's physical throne; David is heir to Christ's spiritual throne. (16)
* Christ is the Morning Star - The dawning of the New Day which will never end. (16)
* The saying coming quickly infers that no one has an excuse. (12)
* The prophecies in the Book of the Revelation are not tamper proof; but neither are they escape proof. (18, 19)
* The Lord still quenches thirst. (17)
* In connection with the saint's invitation to the Lord to come, Paul uses the Syriac term 1 Cor. 16:22 Maranatha meaning "the Lord will come"

The Author and Finisher of Our Faith

HEB. 12:1-13

Introduction:

In chapter 10:35, 36 the writer of this epistle has said: cast not away your confidence which hath great recompence of reward.

For ye have need of patience, that, after ye have done the will of God, ye might receive the promise.

Some of the Hebrew believers had entered their names on the roll of believers but had not moved forward or begun to run. After seeing the length of the course with the stiffness of its gradients and hindrances, they were about to withdraw.

Their attention is drawn to three things by the writer:

* The <u>struggle</u>: (lay aside the weight; some athletes may use weights to train, but afterwards fling them aside; however, love of family, country, and ease can hold them back

* The <u>strategy</u>: looking unto Jesus; looking αφοραω aphorao, looking away from all else the vision of Jesus should thrill the soul, knowing that He has been down this same road

* The <u>spectators</u> in the arena who had run and triumphed with laurels.

● ●

Translation, Transliteration, Interpretation:

1) Compassed about, εχοντες-περικειμαι echontes perikeimai, lying around us with witnesses who testify of their own experiences. Chapter 11

Lay aside, αποθεμενοι apothemenoi, lay off as old clothes

Weight, ογκον ogkon, encumbrances that handicap as doubt, pride, sloth, ungirdedness

Sin, ηαρμαρτιαν harmartian, to miss a mark

Easily beset, ευ περιστημι eu peristemi, easily surrounding, (as wild beasts in the jungle surrounding a camp fire ready to pounce on the unexpecting

Race, αγωνα agona, contest, contention, strife, struggle

2) Author αρχηγον archegon, leader, and pioneer of personal faith

Finisher, τελειοω teleioo, perfecter, consummator

Endured, ηυπομενω hupomeno, to remain, stay behind after others have departed, and bear up under, to suffer patiently

Despising, φρην phren, frame of mind, attitude

Shame, αισχυνης aischunes, disgrace, dishonorableness

3) Consider, αναλογισσσθε analogisssthe gar, consider well

Contradiction, αντιλεγω antilego, gainsaying

Faint, εκλυω ekluo, loosen out, set free, and be tired out

4) resisted, αντικαθιοτημι antikathistemi, stand in opposition, against in battle stand face to face in line of battle

*   Unto blood, as Jesus and others had (ch. 11)

4) Striving, ανταγωνιζομαι antagonizomai, contending

5) Forgotten, εκλανθανω eklanthano, cause to forget

Exhortation, παρακλησις paraklesis, admonish, persuade, plead, entreat Prov. 3:11:12

6) Chasteneth, παιδευω paideuo. Instruction, correction, punishment Eph. 6:4

Scourge, μαστιξ mastix, to whip. (Jesus was scourged Matt. 26:67)

Dealeth, προσφερω prosphero, to bear or bring to, to apply to, νοθος nothos, spurious

9) Reverence, ενετρεπω enetrepo, respected, to turn in or at (Matt. 21:37)

Father of <u>spirits</u>, πνευματων pneumaton, our spirits or souls

10) Pleasure, δοκεω dokeo, seem good

Profit, συμφερω sumphero, bear together (1 Cor. 12:7)

Partakers, μεταλαμβανω metalambano, for the partaking

11) Peaceable fruit, ειρηνη καρπον eirene karpon (Jas. 3:17)

Exercised, γεγυμναζω gegumnazo, disciplined, as in a gymnasium

12) Feeble, ανορθοω anorthoo, as palsied

13) Make straight, ορθος orthos

Lame, χωλον cholon, limping, halting

Hang down, παριημι pariemi, let pass, relax

Out of the way, εκτρω ektro, turn out of joint, to twist

Be healed, ιαθηδε iathede, heal, cure, restore (from state of sin)

• •

Practical lessons:
* Running with a bag of gold is just as heavy as a bag of lead. Both can hold you back. (1)
* The eye of the runner is not to be fixed on the cloud of witnesses but on author/ finisher
* Considering Christ can be a remedy for mental fainting. (3)
* Resisting God rather than sin can mean giving up the race.
* Circumstances in our lives could be worse and might yet be in the future. (4)

* Our striving is to be against sin, not against each other
* There are some things that we should never forget (Prov. 3:11, 12)
* We faint when we: <u>give up</u>, <u>question our sonship</u>, <u>give way to unbelief</u>, <u>dispare</u>, <u>seek self and not God</u> (5)
* Some are hardened by chastisement (8)
* We can fight against <u>chastisement</u> by <u>complaining</u>, <u>criticism</u>, <u>carelessness</u>, <u>callousness</u> (8)
* Chastisement is not always <u>retributive</u> but sometimes <u>corrective</u> and other times <u>preventive</u>: as with David 2 Sam. 22, 23; with Job 42:6; Paul 2 Cor. 12:7; Abraham (cultivating to be friend of God). (7)
* Trusting in Christ is not the finishing post but the starting point. (11, 13)
* The track that we are running on is the same track all run on, and won't be changed just for me.
* The requirement in this race is not speed but discipline
* Each stroke of chastening from God should be taken <u>soberly</u>, <u>sensibly</u>, and <u>spiritually</u>.

Chastening of God demonstrates evidence of Fatherhood and Sonship.

Job 5:17 happy is the man whom God correcteth, therefore despise not the chastening of the Almighty

* Earthly parents fail either by under disciplining, over discipling, failing to discipline, having the wrong motive, disciplining the wrong way, or at the wrong time; this does not describe God. (9 10)
* Running in circles will not get us to God's goal for us.
* Looking back while running subjects the runner to stumbling and falling.
* The weight of the heavy clothes of sin will hold runners back. We must take them off. (Eph. 4:22-24)
* The charge is not to lay aside duty but our besetting sins. (1)
* Laying weights aside is a matter of choice (1)
* <u>Let us</u> implies that we are all charged with this responsibility. (1)

Chastening is not pleasant but it is beneficial, yielding fruit. (11-13)

* The guilty son will see God's loving hand in the chastening and will yield so that the intended result will be realized speedily.
* Travelers may rest and refresh themselves but runners must continue.

Race runners have prerequisites: have <u>rigor</u>, <u>self denial</u>, <u>discipline</u>, <u>perseverance</u>, <u>endurance</u>, <u>exertion</u>

Gal. 5:7 ye did run well who did hinder you that ye should not obey the truth.

Ps. 119:32 I will run the way of thy commandments, when thou shall enlarge my heart.

1Cor. 9:24 know ye not that they which run in a race run all, but one receiveth the prize, so run that ye may obtain

Living With Hope
1 THESS 4:13-5:11

Introduction:

After Paul's journey to Philippi, he voyages to Thessalonica (Acts 17:1-9). This city was populated predominately by Gentiles; but there were quite a few Jews there. It was the capital of Macedonia, and was a trade center, eastward and westward. The city was named by Cassander in honor of his wife around 315 B.C. the religion was idolatry, and devotion was given to Caesar. There was a Jewish Synagogue there into which Paul went upon his arrival. Many Gentiles, women and Jews believed his teaching about Jesus; many Jews rejected him and his teaching. Paul was immediately sent out of town by his friends, leaving Timothy and Silas. (3:1-2). Paul later arrives at Berea, Athens, and then to Corinth where he wrote both of the letters to the Thesselonians, Acts 18:1, 11. Paul had received a letter from Timothy (3:6-13) regarding the condition of the Church there, consequently, Paul writes to commend (3:6), to expose fornication (4:3), to activate idleness (4:11), exhort young converts (4:1-12), to answer false charges (2:3, 9-10, 4-6, 17-20), and to correct misapprehension about the return of Christ. (4:13-17). Paul was hindered from returning (2:17-18)

• •

Translation, Transliteration, Interpretation:

13) Ignorant, αγνοριν agnorin, not known, no advantage

Asleep, κοιμαω koimao, to put to sleep. (Greek, Romans, and Jesus' word for death)

* The dead believers were described to be asleep.

No hope, ελπιδα elpida, hopelessness

Earthly parents fail either by under disciplining, over disciplining, failing to discipline, having the Wrong motive, disciplining the wrong way, or at the wrong time; this does not describe God. (9, 10).

Running in circles will not get us to God's goal for us.

Looking back while running, subjects the runner to stumbling and falling.

The weight of the heavy clothes of sin will hold runners back. We must take them off. (Eph. 4:22-24).

The charge is not lay aside duty, but our besetting sins. (1)

Laying weights aside is a matter of choice. (1)

Let us, implies that we are all charged with this responsibility. (1)

Chastening is not pleasant, but it is beneficial, yielding fruit. (11-13)

The guilty son will see God's loving hand in the chastening and will yield so that the intended result will be realized speedily.

Travelers may rest and refresh themselves, but runners must continue.

Race runners have prerequisites: have rigor, self denial, discipline, perseverance, endurance, and exertion.

Gal. 5:7 Ye did run well; who did hinder you that ye should not obey the truth?

Ps. 119:32 I will run the way of thy commandments, when thou shall enlarge my heart.

1 Cor. 9:24 Know ye not that they which run in a race run all, but one receiveth the prize? So run that ye may obtain

* There were many, then and now who believe that death is the end

15) prevent, φθανω phthano, precede, come before, anticipate

* The 2nd coming of the Lord is called the Parousia; this word described a visit from a dignitary

Archangel, Michael is the only one mentioned (Jude 9)

16) Shout, κελευω keleuo, this was like a military command

Trump, σαλπιγγι salpiggi, this is short for trumpet, blown to gather and alert

First, πρωτον proton (before those who are alive are changed (1 Cor. 15:52)

17) Paul uses the term "we" including himself among those who could be living then caught up, 'αμα, hama at same time. Συν sun, together with 'αρπαζω harpazo, to seize, carry off, rapture

18) Comfort, απαντησιν apantesin, to meet

5:1) Know perfectly, ακριβως οιδατε akribos oidate, accurately know

5:2) Thief, κλεπτης kleptes

5:4) Overtake, καταλαμβανω katalambano, take before

5:5) Children of Day, 'υιοι φωτος huioi photos, sons of Day

Darkness, σκοτους sktous

5:6) Sleep, this sleep is another metaphor, but this time the eyes would be open, this is spiritual lethargy

6) Watch, γυηγορωμεν grenoromen, keep awake

Sober, νηφωμεν nephomen, not to be drunk

Drunken, μεθυσκω methusko, to get drunk

*   Night time is a favorite time for drunken revelries

5:9) Appointed, εθετο etheto (to direct or determined etc.)

11) Edify, οικοδομειτε oikodomeite, to build up

Practical lessons:

* Saints are to be physically and spiritually sober or on guard. (5:6)
* Night time is a common time for sleeping; but also drunkenness (5:5)
* Only the regenerating power of God's Word can quicken to eternal life. (5:6)
* The saints need spiritual armor in this world (5:8)
* The long-term goal of the saints is to be with the Lord. (9-11)
* If we are children of light we should walk in the light. (4-8)
* Those who have not accepted Jesus are without hope or hopeless. (1 Cor. 15:19)
* Christ will descend just as He promised.
* Death is not final; it takes the saints from one world to another. (14)
* Rapture ραπτυς raptus, means to seize, to be caught up
* The unsaved are thinking safety and peace; like Sodom, Gomorrah, and the days of Noah.
* We can not possibly afford to overlook or be overlooked by the rapture. (16-18)
* World complacency is dangerous and detrimental. (5:1-3)
* The day of the Lord came in the Old Testament and is coming again in the New; it is a day of judgement.
* The saints have no grounds for uneasiness. (15)
* Judaism has been called a "this world only" religion.
* Zechariah has predicted that 2/3 of Israel would be slain and becoming for the most parts a large cemetery. (Zech. 13:8, 9)
* The great tribulation will be described as Jacob's trouble. (Jer. 30:6, 7)
* There are reasons for hope at the end of each chapter of 1 Corinthians.
  1) Exemplary hope, 2) motivation hope, 3) purifying hope, 4) comforting hope, invigorating hope

Treasure in Clay Jars

2 COR. 4:2-15

Introduction:

A treasure is something that is highly esteemed to be of great value. It can be of any kind. One man's junk can be another man's gem.

The priceless Hebrew scrolls (scriptures), which had been hidden to preserve them, were found in the Cumran Cave near the Dead Sea in 1947; their value cannot be estimated; they are priceless.

Today we will recognize the treasure that we have in our possesion. The Gospel is often overlooked and under valued.

• •

Translation, Transliteration, Interpretation:

1) We faint not, ουκ εκκακεω ouk ekkakeo, to be fainthearted or to lose spirit

2) Renounced, απειπον apeipon, to refuse, to forbid

* Dishonesty is generally hidden from view

Craftiness, πανουργια panourgia, cunning, to scheme, to plot

Deceitfully, δολουντες dolountes, falsifying, trickery

Commending, συνιστημι sunistemi, favorable attention, to recommend

4) blinded, ετυφλος etuphlos, mental blindness

5) We preach not ourselves (we are not egotists)

6) Light of the knowledge (metaphorical) φοτισμον photismon, radiance, and blaze
* Light of knowledge can be called enlightenment ("...we beheld His Glory ...")

7) treasure, θησαυρος thesauros, precious deposite, receptacle vessel (container)

Excellency, ωπερβολη uperbole, surpassingness

10) Bearing the dying (metaphor)

11) Life mad manifest (metaphor)

12) Death works (metaphor)

13) As it is written (this is a quote from Ps 116:10

14) present us: God will present or display us to the new world

Jesus will present us to the Father

15) Redound, ερισσευση erisseuse, respecting, concerning, apply, glorify

<u>Practical Lessons</u>:
- True saints will not compromise with false teachers. (2)
- God pleasing ministry requires honesty, integrity, and accountability. (2)
- The devil blinds men by false teaching; Christ opens blinded hearts and minds. (3, 4)
- Blinded minds are worst than blinded eyes. (4)
- Our focus should always be on Christ and our goal for God's glory. (5, 6)
- God who commanded the sun to shine out of darkness has shined in our hearts because our hearts were dark. (6)
- God's power is demonstrated in strengthening our weaknesses. (7)
- The treasure in the vessel makes the vessel valuable. (7)
- We should look at difficulties as challenges rather than defeats. (8-10)
- Suffering <u>for Christ</u> assures us of eternal life <u>with Christ</u>. (10-12)
- Satan delivers unto death; Christ delivers from death. (11)
- Our focus should be on the treasure rather than the vessel. (11-12)
- Suffering for Christ encourages others to suffer patiently for God's glory. (15)

Raised to New Life

ROM. 6:1-4, 12-14, 20-23

Introduction:

The lesson today is about life and death; the old life and the new life; physical death and eternal death. It is about Spiritual baptism into Christ by the Holy Spirit of God.

Someone has said that chapter 6 of Romans has no water. Meaning; that the baptism spoken of is Spiritual. Of course, water baptism is a type or simulation of Spiritual baptism in Christ.

Our subject is "raised to new life". The inference here is that the believer has died with Christ, has been buried with Christ, has risen with Christ, and has a continuing relationship with Him.

The believer has been set free from a continuous life of sin.

It is interesting that many prisoners do not want to set free because freedom requires responsibility which is not easy to handle. But our freedom in Christ is managed with the help of the Holy Spirit promised of God and given by Christ. 1 Jn. 3:9 says that we do not continue in sin.

· ·

Translation, Transliteration, Interpretation:

In Rom. 5:20 Paul has been talking about God's grace which does much more abound than sin does. And many may ask that if grace abounds because of sin, should we sin to make sure grace continues to abound?

The question is rhetorical (figurative) and interrogatory. This is the language of verse 1

* It is one thing for sin to continue in us, but quite another for us to continue in sin.
* God's grace in early days was turned into lasciviousness (intemperance) Jude 4

2) Paul answers the question: God forbid, means does not even entertain the thought for a moment

177

* abounding sin is the occasion for abounding grace
* Grace is given to kill sin, not to encourage it
* It is absurd that a medicine should feed the disease it extinguishes
* Death to sin is the consequence of union with Christ
* Sin can flourish anywhere but in the shadow of the Cross of Christ

Abound, πλεοναζω pleonazo, large, much, great

Dead to sin, αποθνησκω apothnesko, to die, rot, putrescent, wither
* How can that which is dead and rotten live any longer?
We have renounced allegiance with sin

3) Baptized into Jesus Christ: this was done by the Holy Spirit (1 Cor. 12:10). This established our union with Christ. This Baptism is like putting on an outer garment, confirming an inner relation
* being baptized into Christ infers participating in His gracious benefits.

4) Buried, συνθαπτω sunthapto, to bury together (as in Vs. 3)

* Burial is the confirmation of death
* Baptism is an exhibition of burial and sealing in death
* Spiritual baptism is the conformity of the members to the head
* Heb. 2:17 Christ was in all things made like unto His brethren. Rom. 8:29 brethren made like Him.
* being raised like Christ is a glorious privilege Col. 2:12
* Our life on earth is a resurrected life Col. 3:1
* walking in newness is: with new principles, decisions, tastes and aims

Raised, ηγειρω egeiro, aroused, awaken, raise from the dead

Newness, καινοτητι kainoteti, differing in character

12) Reign, βασιλευετω basileueto, the regal exercise of authority
* We have the authority to let or hinder the reign of sin in us

Mortal, θνεσκω thnesko, subject to death

In the lusts, επιθυμιαις epithumiais, in the desires

* Believers' cooperation is required in our sanctification Phil. 2:12
* Sin is here personified as king ruling universally over men. (1 Jn. 5:19
Sin exercises dominion over sinners with their consent

Sin may remain as an outlaw, oppress as a tyrant, but cannot reign as king in the saint

13) Yield, παριστημι paristemi, at the disposal, have in readiness, place beside members, μελη mele, a part of a body
* Different members of the body are instruments of different lusts and vices instruments, 'οπλα hopla, armor, weapons, and equipment

Sin, αμαρτια amartia, misses a mark, error, guilt of wrong

* To yield is to voluntary enlist to God as our king
* All offerings to God are useless unless we first offer ourselves (Prov. 3:26)
* Sin shall not have dominion over you: this is a fact, but also a promise
* The Law has only two words: <u>do</u> or <u>die</u>
* We are not under the law so we are not under its curse
* The believer is not under the law, but we are not above it either

* Sinners are not mere servants of sin but slaves to it
* Sin is deceptive with promises and a show of liberty, but its wages are death.

• •

Additional Practical Lessons:
* God's grace is not a pass to sin. (2)
* Believers were once dead in sin, now they are dead to sin. (2)
* Baptism is a public statement. (3, 4)
* Baptism does not give union with Christ but seals it. (3)
* Sin may live in us but we cannot live in sin (2)
* Lust leads into sin. (12)
* Instruments of unrighteousness are weapons of war against God and His Saints. (13)
* The body is a house full of weapons and tools for good or evil.
* Without Christ men's bodies are living coffins carrying dead souls. (13)
* God supplies our gifts but we should stir them up. (2 Tim. 1:6)
* Sin may lodge in the house but cannot be Lord of the house. (12, 14)
* Christ satisfying the law for us removes us from its jurisdiction. (14)

* Saints are open under new management, (14, 20) and are not bound by the guilt of the past.
* Freedom from righteousness is man's greatest misery; freedom in righteousness is man's greatest mercy
* The fruit of unrepentent sin ripens in hell as the fruit of a flower
* Eternal life is not earned but it is a gift. (23)
* Holiness is not the result of law but the liberty of grace. (22)

Under Sin's Power

ROM. 3:9-20

Introduction:

Chapter 3 of Romans begins with descriptions of the ungodly: vs. 3 <u>unbelievers</u>, verse 5 the <u>unrighteous</u>, vs 7 <u>sinners</u>, vs 8 <u>slanderers</u>.

Genesis 6:5 God gives His description: and God saw that the wickedness of man was great in the earth, and that every imagination of the thoughts of his heart was only evil continually.

Romans 1:19-32 shows the indictment against the Gentiles, and 2:17-29 shows the indictment against the Jews.

The Jews advantage worked a greater condemnation for them because they had received God's oracles and the Gentiles were without them; the verdict was: all were guilty

• •

9) Better, προεχομεθα proechometha, in better case, excel to one's advantage, to be prefered

Proved, προαιτιαμαι proaitiamai, laid to the charge, prior to but not merely an accusation

Under sin, ηυππο ηαμαρτι huppo hamartian, influence, causation, subject to (7:14 Gal. 3:22)

Ps. 14:1,3, 140:3, 2 Cor. 6:16; Rom.9:25,27, 11:26,34, 12:19; Isaiah 59:7,8

Paul's reasoning here is to humble the sinner and to exalt the Savour

* The Jews were not superior to the Gentiles in Divine acceptance, but equally liable to God's wrath
* Nominal Christians are no better before God than others.
* Believers differ by grace only 1 Cor. 4:7

* Under sin; its guilt, condemnation, ruling power, unable to free self from it
* A broken law gives sin power over the transgressor Rom. 7:4; 1 Cor. 15:56
* The Jews were convicted of the very law of which they boasted
* Sin is coming short of the purpose for which man was created
* All were children of wrath Eph: 2:3

10) None righteous; <u>total depravity</u>, <u>universal depravity</u>

* Each person is known to God as if the only one in the world

* All of Adam's offspring are involved in his transgression Rom. 5:12, and made in his sinful likeness

11) Understand, συνιων, sunion, to grasp, to comprehend

12) Out of the way, εκκλινω ekklino, to avoid, to turn away from

* gone out of God's way into their own way Isaiah 53:6

Unprofitable, αχρεοω achreoo, not useful, useless as sour milk, or a dead carcass, as bad figs Jer. 24:2, or bad fish Matt. 13:48

13) Sepulchre, ανοιγω anoigo means it is an open grave that stinks. (this is metaphoric)

Tongues, γλωσσα glossa, speech, talk, language, flattery, lies, bribes (metaphoric)

14) Bitterness, πικριας pikrias, harsh (Ps. 10:7)

* Here we can see what Isaiah meant: 1:5 the whole head is sick. (Jer. 8:22 balm in Gilead)
* Even Peter cursed in the Master's presence Matt. 26:74; Mk. 14:7
* Bitterness is like arrows which wound and kill. Ps. 64:3
* cursing is the natural language of a depraved heart.

15) Feet shed innocent blood (this figure of speech is called metonymy) (of the adjunct)

* Blood shed was the first sin committed after the fall
* see Isaiah 59:7

20) Justified, δικαοω dikaoo, accounted righteous, declared righteous

Not by deeds of the law: works of the law, (not set right with God)

• •

Translation, Transliteration, Interpretation: (please see above)

Practical lessons:
* Sin's guilt must be removed before its power can be destroyed. (9)
* Preachers must fortify statements with scripture proofs (9)
* Sin reigns (5:21), enslaves (6:6), rules (6:12), exercises lordship (6:14): victims are enslaved by it (6:16, 17, 20), can be freed from it (6:18, 20)
* Christ makes men legally righteous by imputed righteousness and morally right by His imparted Spirit.

Sin blinds understanding and perverts the will. Sinners call evil good and good evil Isaiah 5:20
* seeking God is the mark of true Godliness. Ps.22:26, 26:8, 104:4
* Natural man will not seek God because God is his enemy (8:7)
* Natural man seeks after vanity rather than after God. (Ps.4:2)
* Grace restores God's image of love, life and truth in man. (12)
* Sin defiles every member of the body, making them instruments of unrighteousness, and needing the Great Physician. (6:12, 13)
* A sinner's words are putrid and his exhilations are of a dead soul. (13)
* Their tongues are as serpents waiting for the prey. (Ps.52:4, 57:4, 64:3)
* The tongue is an unruly member, a fire, a world of iniquity. (Jas.3:6)
* Many practice deceit but are insulted when called liars. They hate in others while practicing the same thing.
* Sins of Vs 13, 14 are the worst kind because hardest to cure (13, 14)
* Sin fits man's feet for Satans' errands. (15)
* Our feet are to be shod with the preparation of the gospel.
* The feet of the righteous are beautiful because they are employed in publishing the gospel of peace Rom. 10:15
* Satan's children bear his murderous image. (Jn. 8:44)
* Men dread God as judge before revering Him as Father. (18)
* God's will is revealed in the Law. (19)
* All Scripture is written for our instruction. Rom. 15:4
* The mouths of sinners will be stopped either here or hereafter

* The guiltiness of mankind is doubled: thru Adam the federal head, and also in personal life
* The law, written on the conscience and heart only discovers sin, doesn't remove it. 2:14, 15
* The statue book acquits of crime but it dosent acquit the criminal
* The law kills so that the gospel can make alive.
* Knowledge of sin dosen't save but no one is saved without it. (20)

Ignoring God's Clear Truth

ROM. 1:18-23, 28-32

Introduction: is the heathen lost? Is it fair that those who never in the lifetime heard or read the gospel message should be eternally condemned?

God's wrath is justly deserved; He has given sufficient knowledge of Himself to induce reverent worship and obedience of Himself: in <u>conscience,</u> and in <u>nature</u>.

When men refuse to recognize and serve God's revealed truth, He then gives them over to their own way.

The gospel cannot save man until he sees himself; guilty, lost, and condemned.

The grave problem facing humanity is not going away until it is properly diagnosed.

Evil is not the result of ignorance, mistreatment, poverty, childhood abuse, or the environment; these factors make it more likely to fall into a corrupt lifestyle; they do not in themselves produce evil. Thinking this way is self delusion.

The real answer is the acknowledgement of the truth and the Author of the Scripture, which fallen man fails to do. There is a way to escape God's wrath. (Rom. 5:9).

Paul's letter to the Romans was written from Corinth during Paul's third journey. Nero was the emperor, just beginning to reign (54-68). Paul's letter is dated around 56 A.D.

The scope of the letter is "God's salvation for sinners" and it spells out the ABCs of the gospel; interpreting the truths already spoken by Jesus.

There was a large Jewish population settled in Rome. The gospel had already been advanced there and Paul was planning to visit the Roman saints there soon. (15:23, 24)

• •

Translation, Transliteration, Interpretation:

18) Wrath, οργανω organo, to teem, to swell; God's Holy displeasure against sin. All evil and rebellion is the object of God's wrath.

Revealed, κατεχοντων katechonton, apokalupto, to uncover or unveil

Hold (the truth), κατεχω katecho, to hold down truth or conceal truth, to conceal

19) Known (of God), γνοστον gnoston, the knowable, the known

Manifest, φανερωσεν phanerosen, make known

Shewed, εφανερωσεν ephanerosen (phanero), cause to appear, evince, manifest

20) Invisible, αορατα aorata (horato), unseen

Clearly, καθοραται kathoratai, to mark, perceive, discern, look down upon.

Understood, νοουμενα nooumena (nous), perceived, intellect

Godhead, θειοτης theiotes, divinity

Excuse, αναπολογητους anapologetous (apologemai excuse

*   There is no true atheist (such a person dose'nt eliminate truth but only covers/ suppresses it)

Knew (God) γνοντες gnontes (gnosko), know by personal experience they had some knowledge of God

21) Vain, ματαιοομαι mataioomai, false, empty, unprofitable

Imagination, διαλογισμος dialogismos, reasoning

Foolish, ασυνετος, asunetos, senseless

Darkened, σκοτιζω skotizo, (unable to put the evidence together about God, darkness settled down in their hearts)

23) Changed, αλλαττω allatto, to alter

Image, εικονος eikonos, copy

24) φθειρω phtheiro, spoil, ruin, perishable, morally depraved (was totally depraved)

28) Retain (refused), δοκιμαζω dokimazo, to reject after trial

Gave over, παρεδωκεν paredoken, withdrawal

*   God left them to work their own wicked way. He released from restraint. Increased freedom to sin

Reprobate, αδοκιμος adokimos, disapproved,

Not convenient, καθηκοντα kathekonta, not seemly or comely, shameful, unnatural, leading to polly-theism (See 1 Cor.9:27; 2 Cor.13:5-7) (as an abandoned bldg. Full of bats, & snakes)

29) Malignity, κακοηθιας kakoethias, build a bad construction of things

Whisperers, ψιθυριζω psithurizo, speak secretly into the ear

30) Back biters, καταλαλους katalalous, talking back

Inventors, εφευρετας epheuretas, one who finds out (something) more

31) Without natural affection (homosexual, slave trade, sacrificing babies, etc)

• •

Practical Lessons:
*   Sin hinders progress of truth; truth is never completely destroyed, only kept back/ hidden 18)
*   Knowledge of God's revelation is sufficient to restrain from idolatry and vice. (18)
*   Truth is open but wicked men put it in a box with a lid on it to conceal it
*   Our sin is our choice. (18, 19)
*   The heart may be home of the Holy Spirit or the home of evil desires. (Mk. 7:21; Rom.1:21)
*   Insensibility to Divine goodness is the beginning of apostasy. (20)
*   Some philosophers profess to be wise but have become fools. (22)
*   Some men create their own idols. (21, 23)
*   When men become reprobate God leaves them to wallow in their own filthiness. (28)
*   God's wrath is not confined to the past but is still being revealed from heaven. (18)
*   To attempt to replace truth with foolishness is the height of arrogance which invites God's wrath (21, 22)

* All Creation constitutes a school of theology for man
* perverted reason either doesn't see or draws false conclusions. (20)
* God is dishonored when His works are worshipped rather than He, the Creator. (20)
* God's wrath is no sudden temporary emotion or burst of passion. (18)
* His wrath is revealed and His justice written on man's conscience to show man's spiritual need
* Truth is chained in the prison of man's corruption.; it must either expel sin or be expelled.
* A wicked heart is the dungeon where truth is held captive. (18)
* Idolatry is the epitome of utter foolishness. (23)
* Those who cannot control their appetite for sin are dragged down to a miserable greater judgment.
* Be careful not to sin by condoning the evil of others. (32)

Teaching God's Word

ACTS 18:1-11

Introduction:

Paul had been waiting for Timothy and Silas to arrive from Macedonia. He had left them there to train the many new converts gained there. Paul was already disappointed in Athens because of, idolatry; now he goes to Corinth and finds something much worse.

Corinth was about 50 miles from Athens. It was known for its idolatry and immorality.

The city had been destroyed about 200 years before Paul's time and rebuilt by Julius Caesar in 44 B.C. and then settled by Roman colonists. This city was better known as "sin city".

There were at least a thousand cult prostitutes with very loose morals.

Paul would have little success in the Synagogue of the Jews and not much more in the market place. He had not seen this level of idolatry before. (17:16)

• •

Translation, Transliteration, Interpretation:

2) Aquila may have been a freed man as many Jews in Rome were. He was born in Pontus which is today called turkey. Paul may have met Aquila in the Synagogue.

Aquila and His wife Priscila had lived in Rome but had left with other Jews who had been ejected by Cladius Caesar because the Jews were in a state of constant Tumult.

Tiberius caesar had already deported about four thousand earlier. There were about 20,000 Jews living in Rome.

Commanded, διατάσσω diatásso, to dispose, arrange

3) Same craft, ‘ομοτέχνον homotechnon, of the same trade or occupation

189

Tentmakers, οκήυη πόιεω skéne póieo. Tents were made of leather or animal hide. See Acts 18:18, 26, 20:34; 1 Cor. 16:19; Rom. 16:3. Paul had moved in with them.

4) Reasoned, διελόγετο dielógeto, converse, exchange ideas

Persuaded, επέιθεν epéithen, peitho, to convince, to pacify

5) Pressed, συνειχέτο suneicheto, held together; some say this word does not mean depressed but rather constrained (impressed) by the Holy Spirit. See 1 Cor. 2:3

* Paul did not use enticing words but gave the truth from the Law, prophets, and the Writings. No doubt he told of his Damascus experience.

Silas and Timothy finally arrived with gifts of support from Philippi. (1 Thess. 3:16; 2 Cor 11:9; Phil 4:15

6) opposed themselves, αυτιτασσω autitasso, in battle array, face to face See Rom. 13:2; Jas.4:6; 1 Pet.1:5. They blasphemed and railed against Paul

Shook, εκτινάσσω (ektinasso), to shake out, or shake off

* This same word is used in Matt. 10:15, Mk. 6:11 regarding shaking the dust off of the feet

Own heads, κεφάλην kephalen, the head (See Matt27:25, 23:35; Eze.3:18, 33:4 2 Sam. 1:16

Clean, καθαρος katharos, pure from your blood, unsoiled, guiltless (Rom. 11:25)

To the Gentiles, Eph.19:1-10; Rom.28:23-28

7 Justus, there were several men with this name, Barnabus, Acts 1:23 and Jesus, called Justus, Col. 4:11

This Justus was in the pottery business in Corinth.

8) Crispus, Paul had baptized Him (1 Cor. 1:14). Silas and Timothy did most of the baptizing.

9) Be not afraid, μη φοβου me phobou, σιωπησης siopeseis, stop being afraid

Speak, λαλέο laleo, go on speaking

Hold not thy peace, μη σιωπάω me siopao, hold not your peace

10) Set on thee, επιθη'σεται epithesetai, to lay, throw self upon, to attack 8 this is not the word <u>sit</u> on but <u>set</u> on

11) 18 months, Paul had been there for some time before "continuing". Perhaps he was there 2yrs. Or more in the city and around about. 2 Cor. 11:10; Rom.16:1

• •

Practical lessons:
* Teaching must go on after the preaching is over. (1-4) Matt. 28:19, 20
* Many people look for a Saviour but refuse Jesus who is the Saviour because He is not what they were expecting. (5)
* we must not spend all of our time on hard hearted people but move on to those who are more open to the gospel. (6)
* Those who truly seek God are ready when they see the light of the gospel. (7)
* God's power produces the strongest protection available to us. (9-11)

The words teach in our subject is:
In Hebrew yada עַדְיְ cause to know, yarah הֲרָיְ show direct
In Greek κατηχεω katecheo to instruct
Παιδευοω paideuoo to train

Making God Known

ACTS 17:1-4, 10-12, 22-25, 28

Introduction:

In the lesson today, Paul has arrived at Thessalonica. This city earlier had been named Solonika, later it was called Therma because it was at the head of the Thermatic gulf. Then Cassander renamed it Thessalonica after his wife who was sister of Alexander the Great.

Thessalonica was the capital of the province of Macedonia and it shared commerce from the Agean Sea with Ephesus and Corinth.

Paul tells us (1:8) that this was the strategic center for the spread of the gospel. This city was the spring board of the gospel in Asia Minor.

There was only one Synagogue there, illustrating the scarcity of the Jews there.

While in the city Paul received help from the City of Philippi (Phil.4:16). Paul worked night and day to support himself.

• •

Translation, Transliteration, Interpretation:

2) Paul's custom on arrival in a new city was first to enter the Synagogue and speak with the Jews. This was also Jesus' custom.

3 Sabbath days, this no doubt included week days also. The rest of the time he spoke outside of the Synagogue. .

Reasoned, διαλεγομαι dialegomai, to converse, exchange ideas

Out of the scriptures, the law, the prophets, and the writings were Pauls' basis.

3) Alleging, παρατιθεμενος paratithemenos, to place along side

* 1 Cor. 1:23 a stumbling block to the Jews and foolishness to the Greeks.

Must needs, δει dei, it behoved, it was binding

To suffer, παθειν pathein

* Paul spoke as an eye witness

4) Consorted, προσκληροω proskleroo, to assign by lot (an assignment by God's grace)

Devout, σχομενων schomenon, God fearers

* These were less under the control of the jealous Rabbis and reporting to Paul more readily

Chief women, γυνωκων gunokon, πρωτων proton, first in rank

* These may have been Jewish wives of Gentiles. Not all of the women were high ranking

* Paul and Silas had been hiding because of the danger of the unbelieving Jews. Acts 17:5 so they were probably escorted to get out of town by the Gentile converts.

10) Berea was about 50 miles southwest and was another Macedonian district.

11) Noble, ευγενης eugenes, well born, of good birth

Readiness of mind, προθυμος prothumos, eagerness, rushing forward

Searched, ανακρινω anakrino, examined, careful research, to sift up and down Acts 4:9, 12:19

12) Honorable women, ευσχημονων euschemonon, graceful

* The Jews in Berea sent a messenger to Paul with financial aid for Jerusalem (20:4)

* The unbelieving Jews heard what was going on in Berea and came to stir up the people (13)

15) Paul travels to Athens and waits for Silas and Timothy (15, 16)

22) Mar's Hill, αεροπαγυς aeropagus, market place

Superstitious, δεισνδαιμων deisidaimon, more religious than usual, too religious

23) Unknown God, αγνωστο θεο agnosto Theo

*   Just in case we missed one
*   You are already worshiping Him in ignorance

Declare, καταγγελλω kataggello, to set forth

24) Dwell, κατοικεω katoikeo, to settle down (See Acts 7:48 for Stephen's sermon)

25) Needeth, προσδεομαι prosdeomai, to want besides

28) In God is ζωμεν zomen, life

Κινουμεθα kinoumetha, movement
Εσμεν esmen, existence

Practical lessons:
*   We should search the scriptures to see for ourselves. (11)
*   Preaching ought to make Bible students of the hearers. (11)
*   There should be no private interpretation of the scriptures. 2 Pe.1:20
*   All men are God's offspring. (25)
*   The gospel was given to the Jews, but they still need to hear its message today. (1, 2)
*   The Old Testament scriptures prove the need of Jesus' death and sacrifice. (3, 4)
*   We should be very concerned about rightly dividing God's Word. (3,4,11), 2 Tim.2:15
*   People can be very religious without knowing the true God. (22, 23)
*   God created man and cannot be confined by man. (24, 25)
*   We can make God known by preaching, teaching, and living the gospel.
*   There are some people that cannot be reasoned with. (Isaiah 1:18)

Spreading the Word
ACTS 16:1-5, 8-15

Introduction:

Paul, Barnabas and John Mark had made their first missionary journey together. John Mark had left them fearfully and returned to Jerusalem. After Paul and Barnabas returned and rested for a while they decided to continue evangelizing abroad. There was friction about taking Mark with them again, so they separated. Barnabas took Mark and went in a different direction from Paul. Acts 15:36-39.

In the meanwhile, Judas and Silas, both prophets, having had returned to Antioch with Paul and Barnabas from Jerusalem with confirmation from the Church, tarried at Antioch for a while. (33) Judas goes back to Jerusalem but Silas decides to remain at Antioch. (34)

After the separation of Barnabas, Paul decides to take Silas with him on the second tour. (40) Paul and Silas return to Lystra and Derby where Paul had preached before. This is where Paul meets Timotheus.

Timothy was probably a native of Lystra (2 Tim. 1:5, 6) his mother was Eunice, his grandmother was Lois. All that is mentioned of his father is that he was Greek. He may have been a Jewish proselyte but Timothy was taught the gospel by his mother and grandmother. (2 Tim. 3:15)

Timothy was probably a teenage convert from Paul's first visit to Lystra. Twelve years later, 1 Tim. 1:2, 4:12, Paul seems to spiritually adopt him to replace John Mark.

• •

Translation, transliteration, interpretation:

1) Disciple, μαθητης mathetes, a student, trainee, learner, follower

2) Timothy had a good reputation in the city of Lystra among the Church members.

3) Paul circumcised him: Paul had resisted circumcision of Titus (Gal. 2:3-5) because Gentile liberty was at stake. But Timothy was both Jew and Greek and would continually give offence to the Jews in his ministry, with no advantage to Gentile freedom. See 1 Cor. 9:22

So here for expediency sake, because of the Jews Paul voluntarily circumcised him to remove the stumbling block from Timothy's ministry.

* Here was a question of efficient service not an essential of salvation. He circumcised because of <u>Jewish unbelief</u> not because of <u>Jewish belief</u>.

4) The decrees, δογματα dogmata dokeo to give an opinion (17:7: Lk. 2:1; Col. 2:14) the decrees were the conclusions of the Jerusalem conference. A charter of Gentile freedom of which Silas was witness to. (15:22, 27, 32) the Church was to keep this charter of liberty for continual living rather than temporary.

8) Passing thru, παρελθοντες Parelthontes, without preaching there, <u>down to Troas</u>.

* We can tell that this is where Luke began to travel with Paul and Timothy by the "we" and "they" wording of Vs. 4, 6, 7, 8 and Vs, 10, 11 etc. Paul came here 2 more times 2 Cor.2:12; Acts 20:6

* Twice the Holy Spirit hindered and forbid Paul from going his own way. (Vs. 6, 7)

9) <u>Stood</u> man, ην ηεστως en hestos, histemi, was standing.

Help us, βοηθησον boetheson boetheo, to run at a cry to help

* This was Europe's cry for help

10) Endeavored, εζητ'ησαμεν ezetesamen, we sought

Gathering, συνβιβοζοντες sunbibozontes sunbibazo, concluding, knit together.

11) Loosing from, αναχθαντες anachthantes, setting sail

Straight course, συθυδρομεω euthudromeo, sailing before the wind

12) Phipippi, this city was named after Philip the second, Alexander the Great's father.

* Octavious had planted a colony of Roman veterans here (a military out post)

This city had only a few Jews and not enough (10) to establish a Synagogue.

13) Was want, ενομιζόμεν enomizomen, there was a place for prayer

*   Josephus says that there was a place on the sea coast allowed for the Jews to pray.

14) Lydia was a business woman from Thyatira. Rev. 2:18 this was one of the 7 Churches of Asia.

Lydia sold either the purple dye πορφυρα porphura, or the purple clothing.
The women that were with her were probably her employees.

15) Opened her heart, διηνοιξεν dienoixen, open wide as 2 sides of a folding door.

• •

Practical lessons:
*   It is a wise precaution of the local Church to license and ordain a preacher to verify and confirm his ministry. (2)
*   If God has called a man for His work it will be manifest to others. (2)
*   Many Church members have felt the call from God but received no endorsement from the leaders (3)
*   avoid offending those you intend to evangelize. (3) (1 Cor. 9:22)
*   Knowing the truth of God's grace will strengthen the Church. (4, 5)
*   The Holy Spirit will hinder and prevent His followers from going their own way. (6, 7)
*   Paul's frequent visions always came at a crisis. (At Damascas, at Sea, in Macedonia, etc.)
*   When we understand God's revelations we should follow them. (10)
*   When God commands us we should make a straight course to obey Him. (11)
*   Do not always look to evangelize with people of your own persuasion. (9, 12)

Paul became a "New Alexander" coming to conquer Europe for Christ, and a "New Caesar" to build for Christ.
Jesus deserved the purple robe that Herod put on Him (in mockery) because He is King of the World.

Breaking Down Barriers

ACTS 10:24-38

Introduction:

Our lesson today is about prejudicial barriers in the life of the Christian that must be broken down. God's purpose was that Abraham's seed was to be a blessing to all people. Gen 12:3 See Gal. 3:16; Isaiah 53, 49:6; Acts 13:47.

Cornelius, κορνηλιος in the lesson is believed to be a Proselyte, convinced of the truth but not admitted to full entry into the Jewish faith. (10:37) His name means "of a horn"

He became the firstfruits of a vast Gentile Christian harvest.

Cornelius was one of many Roman Centurions that were prominent in the gospel:

Luke 7:7-8 this Centurion's servant was healed by Jesus. He had built a Jewish Synagogue.

Matt 27:54 this Centurion was convinced of Jesus' innocence (Luke 23:47)

Acts 23:45 Paul used this Centurion in convincing for Roman protection (Acts 22:45)

Acts 23:23 a Centurion accompanied Paul to Caesarea.

Acts 27:43 a Centurion spared Paul in a ship wreck

Acts 28:16 another Centurion confined Paul under house arrest

Cornelius obviously had worked his way up thru the ranks to become a Centurion and placed in Caesarea because of the restlessness of the Jews there.

He was devoted to God. (10:2) having had a vision from God to send for Peter, 30 miles away. In the mean while Peter is in a trance for the same purpose.

• •

Translation, transliteration, interpretation:

5) Call for, fetch μεταπεμπω metapempo, send for another for one's own sake

7) Two servants were sent with one devoted soldier

10) Trance, εκστασις ekstasis, passed out of himself

* This was not the same as a vision ηοραμα horama

15) In the vision God has cleaned the animals up. It took three times to convince of this.

14) Unclean, ακαθαρτον akatharton, unclean

* It seems that Peter was defiling what God had cleaned

17) Peter doubted in himself, διαπορεω diaporeo

20) Get thee down, καταβηθι katabethi

Nothing doubting, μηδεν διακρινομενος meden diakrinomenos a divided mind to waver, Jas. 1:6

22) Just, δικαιας dikaias, righteous

Good report, μαρτυρουμενος marturoumenos, well reported

23) Lodged them, εζεμισεν ezemisen

28) Peter had translated the trance correctly (from animals to man)

29) Gainsaying, αναντιρρητως anantirrhetos, anti= back, against, in return+ phetos to speak _ without answering back

* Peter was guilty of gainsaying with God but this was because of unbelief, what intent, τινι λογωι tini logoi, for what reason

Cornelius commends Peter for breaking away from Jewish tradition to come

34) Of a truth, _____ ep aletheias

* After entering Cornelius' house Peter sees this new great Truth

35) Acceptable, δεχομαι dechomai

36) Lord of all, παντων κυριος panton kurios (Lord of both Jew and Gentile)

37) Peter assumes that Cornelius had heared the main facts about Jesus

• •

Practical Lessons:
* No mere man is to be worshipped. (Nor angels)
* God planned salvation for all men (27-29)
* God reveals Himself to all who seek Him. (39-32)
* God provides what we need to know Him better. (33)
* God accepts anyone who fears Him with reverence. (34, 35)
* Church members have all kinds of barriers to break down, both internal and external
* Christ broke down the barrier of sin. (Eph. 2:14)
* God has established some barriers which He doesn't want broken down.

In the lesson today: preaching was anticipated (10:24-29)

Prayer was answered (10:30-33)

Peace was announced (10:34-36)

Witnessing to the Truth

ACTS 5:27-29, 33-42

Introduction:

The early Church was forewarned by the Lord that it would be persecuted. (Jn. 15:20) Jesus promised that their reward would be great in heaven (Matt. 5:10-12). Even Paul, the Apostle, related to Timothy that all who live Godly would suffer persecution. (2 Tim. 3:12)

In the lesson today, the apostles had been arrested again and put in jail. This was not their first time (4:3). This time they were locked up in the common prison with guards outside the doors. Miraculously, the angel of the Lord opened the prison doors, letting them out and evidently relocked the doors, commanding them to return to the Temple and teach the people. (5:20). When the council sent for them the next day they found the prison cells empty and the guards still outside the doors on guard. (22, 23).

The officials found them teaching in the Temple.

• •

17) The Sadducees had been filled with indignation, ζηλου zelou (zeo) to boil this was primarily because of their disbelief of the resurrection which was being taught.

28) They were interrogated again.

You have filled Jerusalem with your doctrine and intend to bring this man's blood on us.

* They were too evil to call Jesus' name. They had placed Jesus' blood on themselves. Matt. 27:25

29) Ought, δει dei, we must, we have no choice, it is a moral necessity

* These were standing in the same place where Peter and John stood before. (4:20)

33) Cut, διαπρω diapro, to saw in to. They were the same way with Stephen 7:54

34) "Gamaliel" means "reward of God"

* He was teacher of the apostle Paul (22:3) a conservative, with an opposing view from the Sadducees

* Some of the Pharisees were members of the Church, tho untaught & ignorant

35) Take heed, προσεχετε prosechete, hold your mind on yourselves

36) Theu-Das (theodosus), an insurrectionist

400 men joined themselves, προσκλινω prosklino, leaned toward, inclined scattered, δια-σκορπιζω skorpizo, to disperse

37) Judas of Gal-i-lee.

Josephus, the historian, tells us that this Judas created an opposition regarding the taxing.

This was during Quirinius' second visit to Syria. (The 2nd enrollment)

38) Refrain, απιστεμι aphistemi, causing to depart from

Gamaliel had a hands' off policy; not that he was favorable to the Apostles.

Come to naught, καταλυω katalutho; loosen down as a falling house

39) If of God, ει δε εκ θεου εστιν ei de ek theou estin

Cannot be overthrown, καταλυσαι katalusai

41) Counted worthy, καταξιοω kataxioo, to be counted worthy

Suffer shame, ατιμος atimos, to make dishonored

Practical lessons:

* Our doctrine (teaching) of Christ is commanded and we should fill the cities with it. (28)

* Jesus' blood was voluntarily self-inflicted on and by the Jews at the crucifixion. Matt. 27:25

* Obedience to God is definitely preferable to obedience to man. (29)

* We should seize every opportunity to preach and teach the resurrection of Jesus. (29)

* being a truthful witness for God may offend anger, enrage, and provoke some to kill. (33)

* Often God uses ungodly men to assist, preserve, and deliver His people. (34)

* Just because a movement claims to be of God dosent mean it is so. (39)

* The success of a movement doesn't mean God has endorsed it. (39) 2 Thess. 2:10, 11, 12

* God will identify His people by their fruits.

* Enduring persecution is a good sign of our faithful commitment to God. (41)

Sharing All Things

ACTS 4:34-5:10

Introduction:

In the early development of the Church, Luke tells us that the multitude was of one heart and of one soul. (Acts 4:32). But we find in the lesson that Satan entered the heart of two of its members.

• •

Translation, Transliteration, Interpretation:

32) Common, κοινα koina, together, with, in possession and use (2:44)

* Earlier the term meant <u>unclean</u> (10:15)

33) Gave witness, αποδιδοσαν apodidosan, give or pay back a debt, give ones' witness

Great grace, μεγα χαρις mega charis, God's abounding grace

34) Lacked, ενδης endees, poor, needy

Prices, τιμας timas, values

36) Barnabas' was nick name for Joseph, a Levite from Cyprus, meaning son of consolation)

5:1) one of the members of the Church was named <u>Ananias</u>, meaning "God is gracious"

* This was a common name (Acts 9:10, 23:2)

5:2) Kept back, ενοσφισατο enosphisato, to retain

* The property may have sold for more than anticipated; but all was promised to the Church

Privy, συνειδυιας suneiduias, being aware

5) gave up ghost, εκψυχω ekpsuco, breath out, expire

* This was God's judgement. Peter's awareness of Ananias' lie came from God.

6) Wound up, συστελλω sustello, wrap around, draw together, roll together, contract

* This was a quick burial. The men may have used their own mantles.

The quick burial may have been in order to avoid defilement

7) 3 hours later; this time element may not be significant; however, numerologically, theologically, the number infers completion, the end of their foolishness, and God's patience

* Peter may have pointed to the pile of money as He questioned her.

8) agreed together, συμφωνεω sumphoneo, voice together

9) Tempt, πειρασαι peirasai, (Deut. 6:16; Matt. 4:7; Luke 4:12; Prov. 19:9)

Feet, ποδες podes peter probably heard the foot steps of the men from the burial

The men who buried her husband were not present to see her fall.

• •

Practical Lessons:
* God has given the Church the resources it needs to take care of its own. (35)
* We should look for ways to give to the Church to meet the needs of the family of God. (36, 37)
* Ananias could not stand all the praise going to Barnabas rather then him.
* He wanted unlimited dividends with limited investments. (2)

New Power to Proclaim the Truth

ACTS 2:1-13

Introduction:

Our lesson today takes place 50 days after the Passover. It is another Hebrew feast day. Many Jews had remained in Jerusalem from celebrating the Passover 6 weeks prior.

Before ascending Jesus had commanded that the disciples remain in the city until they would be clothed with the Holy Ghost. This was the promise of the Father. (Luke 24:49) Tiberius is the Caesar; Pilate the Governor; and Caiphus, the Chief Priest. Luke records, probably from Rome around 61 A.D. (Acts 28:30).

There are about 120 disciples in the upper room. (Acts 1:15)

• •

Translation, transliteration, interpretation:

1) Fully, συμπληροω sumpleroo, to fill completely

One accord (same place) 'υμου homou, together at same time, likeminded

2) Suddenly, αφνω aphno, unexpectedly

Wind, πνοη pnoe (pneo), air in motion (see John 3:5-8)

*   Wind generally is a symbol of destruction; but here it is a symbol of construction

Sitting, καθημαι kathemai, to sit

*   It seems, they were sitting and the Holy Spirit was sitting upon them.

Sound, ηχος echos, noise, roar

*   Here was an audible sign, followed by a visible sign.

206

3) Cloven, διαμεριζω diamerizo, to divide into parts or pieces, distributing

* As of fire (Jesus had predicted, Acts 1:5). It looked like a single fire, then parting.

4) filled, πληρoω pleroo, to be wholly occupied, (with refining energy)

Tongues, γλωσσαι glossai

* There is no evidence that this gift continued After Apostolic Times Nor in the later times of the apostles themselves. (1Cor.13:1 prophecies would cease, knowledge received by immediate supernatural power would cease, and tongues would cease.

Tongues were not for edification, or instruction or collective guidance but for unbelievers

Utterance, αποφθεγγεσθαι apophtheggesthai, words, to speak, to declare

* Here was an example of eager elevated impassioned utterance (untaught other than native)

5) Devout, ευλαβεις eulabeis, reverent (eu = well, lambano = take, give up self)

6) Confounded, συνχεω suncheo, to pain together (com = together, fundere = pour, for other uses of this word see Acts 9:22, 19:32, 21:27, 31

Galilaeans, which spoke rude, unsophisticated, crude Aramaic (or Greek)

Our own tongue, διαλεκτοι dialektoi, peculiar language of a nation see Jn. 1:46, Acts 4:13

13) New wine, γλευκους gleukous, sweet wine

* Our word glucose; meaning a kind of sugar from fruits, or syrup made from starch

• •

History:

The risen Jesus was seen some 40 days after the resurrection, til 10 day before Pentecost

Maybe Jews had learned to speak other languages (Alexandria Egypt), the miracle was in that every listener heard in His own language

This is said to be the birthday of the Church

The 120 disciples had come down from the upper room and entered the Temple court where many Jews had gathered for observance of the feast.

These 15 Nations that witnessed this event represented much of the Roman Empire.

These locations were included in some of Paul's journeys, and in Peter's 2 letters, 1 Pet. 1:1, 2 Pet. 3:1

Tongues were for signs to the unbeliever. 1 Cor. 14:22

Tongues were: intellectible, personal, universal, comprehensive, purposeful, glorifying

• •

Practical lessons:
The Pentecostal language was a reversal of the confusion of tongues at Babylon Gen. 11:9

* Be not drunk with wine, but be filled with the Spirit.....Eph. 5:18
* Faith commeth by hearing, and hearing by the Word of God. Rom. 10:17
* The gospel was to be preached to the Jew first and also to the Greek Rom. 1:16
* Our speaking should include the wonderful works of God. (11)
* Herein was proof that the Holy Spirit had come to carry on the work of Christ and a New Dispensation Jn. 1:17
* Unknown tongues were not to be spoken without an interpreter. 1 Cor. 14:27, 28

God's Spirit enables us to speak for Him. (4)
God's truth proclaimed in the power of the Holy Spirit provokes wonder and inquisition. (5-8)
No group is unreachable with truth. (9-11)
Even the miraculous proclaiming of truth will be met with scoffing and skepticism. (12, 13)
All believers can be filled with the Spirit, and get refills.

A Wedding in Cana

JOHN 2:1-12

Introduction:

Today we have another lesson about weddings. This one is in Canaan of Galilee which is about 9 miles north of Nazareth. Canaan was the home of Nathanael (Jn. 21:2)

Jesus would perform His first miracle here after which He would later become a gazing stock, jostled by vulgar crowds, spied on from place to place, treated as a public menace, provoked by jealous religious leaders, and seized as a criminal.

In all wedding plans there is always room for embarrassing errors: someone in the party is late, the attire won't fit

The photographer's date's wrong

The cake wasn't delivered

The best man misplaced the ring

Such was the case with this wedding

• •

Interpretation:

1) The third day, this would be three days after Jesus had selected 6 disciples where John the Baptist preached: Andrew, Simon, Philip, Nathaniel, James and John.

Mary was there, maybe as a relative or close friend. She may have helped with arrangements.

2) Jesus was invited with His disciples (invited probably by Mary Jesus' mother)

3) They ran out of wine

Mary tells Jesus: she expected Him to do something

Since she knew of His Divinity and Power

She is probably thinking or ordering as His mother

Mary's husband is not mentioned perhaps because he had died

209

Jesus already knew because of His omniscience

4) Woman, this was a mild rebuke. It wasn't the only time He used this expression. Here He spoke to her as a representative of all rather than as His mother

What have I to do with thee, what do we have in common?

Mine hour is not yet come Jn. 7:6, 8, 30, 3:20 (later He would announce it); 12:23, 13:1, 17:1

5) Do it, here Mary would act as a believer rather than a mother, and Jesus would then comply.

* wedding feasts often lasted for seven days or more so there had to be much to eat and drink

6) Six water pots (the Number 6 is significant)

Purifying, Mk. 7:3, 4 relates that the Jews didn't eat or drink except they wash hands and vessels
See Isaiah 1:22 and Lam. 4:1

Firkin, some say this equaled about 9 gallons, others say a firkin equaled about 20 gallons

7) They filled the pots to the brim (the servants must have wondered how water would solve the problem.)

* The servants would render much service: <u>filling the pots</u>, <u>drawing off</u>, <u>taking to the Governor.</u>

What lessons can we learn from this event?

● ●

Practical Lessons:
* Here we can see the illustration of the failure of Judaism: "Whom ye know not" John 1:26 His own received Him not

* Judaism would be set aside for the birth of Christianity. Gal. 4:4; Lk. 16:16; Jn. 1:35-37

* Judaism still existed but it was cold, having no comfort and giving no joy in their espousal

* Jesus seems to have endorsed the wedding with His presence and His contribution (2)

* We would do well to invite the Lord to share in our joy. (2)

* We can participate in the world's activities without becoming a part of its evil system.

* We have no special claim on God's power as Mary thought she had on Jesus. (3)

* God is both the cause and the effect of change; man is only the means and the instrument (8)

* We should follow the Lord's instructions and He will do the rest. (5)

* Man's worldly religion is worthless to save sinners. (6)

* The condition of natural man is empty. (6)

* God always gives more than enough to accomplish. (7) Phil. 4:19

* Followers of the Lord know how to reach out in troubled times. (5)

* Wonderful things happen when we are <u>on the way</u>. (8) As the 10 lepers

* Regeneration is a Spiritual change of the heart as this physical change of the water.

* Wine is a symbol of the blood of Jesus. Matt. 26:28; 1 Cor. 11:25

* Speaking of the good wine being served first, this is a picture of sin, it looks good at first but its wages are death, which comes at the end.

The best is yet to come. First the Cross then the crown. See Prov. 4:18

* O taste and see................ (9) Ps. 34:8

* God's servants know where the change comes from. (9)

* There is nothing inferior with God. (10)

* Christ's presence is essential for a happy marriage. (2)

Increasing Faith

LUKE 17:1-10

Introduction:

Our lesson today is a continued study of faith. Jesus' apostles asked Jesus to increase their faith; Jesus then began an oration regarding offences, repentance, forgiveness, and servanthood.

• •

Translation, Transliteration, Interpretation:

1) Impossible, ανενδεκτος anendektos, inadmissible, unallowable

Offenses, σκανδαλα skandala, occaision of stumbling, our derivitive of trap/snare

Woe, ουαι - δε ouai - de, a calamity, alas

2) Better, λυσιτελης lusiteles (luo), to pay, well, profitable

*   It is better than facing God with the guilt of ruining one of His little ones

Mill stone, μυλικος λιθος mulikos lithos, a stone used in a mill for grinding.

About, περικειμαι perikeimai, to place around

Little ones, μικρωρ τουτων mikron touton, perhaps young in faith, needing teaching immature

*   Romans 14:13 let us not therefore judge one another anymore:

But judge this rather, that no man put a stumbling block or an accaision to fall in his brother's way.

3) Take heed: this expression points backwards and forward; backward to "cast into the sea" and forward to forgiveness of the trespasser.

Trespass, ημαρτηι hamartei, miss a mark, in error, guilt of wrong

Rebuke, επιτιμαω epitimao, reprove, chide, admonish, and assess a penalty

Forgive, seven times a day (Matt. 18:22) 70 x 7 (Matt. 6:12 forgive our debts as we forgive.)

* 1 Cor. 13:4 charity suffers long....

Don't nurse a grudge or keep score of offenses. Don't be selfishly oversensitive, we are to help others stay right with God and others
God is both the object and the source of faith

5) Increase our faith: this request presupposes;

1) They had faith already
2) They recognized it wasn't strong enough
3) They recognized where faith comes from

7-9) Jesus asks 3 questions regarding servants: would anyone treat a servant as if he is master; does anyone pay the servant before he finishes; does anyone thank the servant for being a servant.

* Then Jesus answers His own questions saying, "I dont think so"

10) After a servant does his job, he's still a servant.

• •

Practical lessons:
* In this world we will definitely offend and be offended. (1)
* Offenses in this world are unavoidable, but those who give or receive them are responsible.
* Offenses are stumbling blocks but even stumbling blocks can be instruments used by God for His purpose of sanctification of His servants. (1)

* Offenses of the wicked proceed from perverse and malignant hearts. The righteous should not always be surprised but expect them. (1)

* If the right-hand or the right-foot (which represent a close friend) offend thee, separate thyself. (1)

* There is great guilt in ruining another's life. (1, 2)

* Dont allow your liberty to become a stumbling block to the weak. (1 Cor. 8:13)

* A life without temperance can easily become a stumbling block. (Gal. 5:23)

* We do not have to wait until the offender repents before having a forgiving spirit. (3)

* God will help us to forget and forgive if we want Him to. (3)

* The parable of the unjust stewart is a good example of forgiveness and its failure. (Matt. 18:22-35)

* It is great folly to refuse mercy while we ourselves need it. (4)

* Love, like its author never grows weary in forgiving. (1 Cor. 13:4) it suffers long. (4)

* To repent honors the penitent rather than disgrace him. (4)

* If we confess our sin God is faithful to forgive..... (1 Jn. 1:9) revenge is deceitful sweetness. (4)

* They who ask for faith show their faith by asking, (5)

* Faith in God surmounts stumbling blocks and freely forgives sin. (5)

* Prayer owes its birth to faith, and faith owes it's increase to prayer. (5)

* All things are possible to him that believeth. (Mk. 9:23)

* With strong faith, offenses fall harmless against believers as water against a rock. (5)

* As servants, don't expect a reward while your task on earth remains unfinished. (8)

* Obedience is no cause for self praise. (10)

* It is not enough to begin a good work; a servant must finish the work for his reward. (10)

* God hensforth calls His servants friends. (Jn. 15:15)

* There is a difference between a debt and a gift. We are His servants; He doesn't owe us but is giving good and perfect gifts every day; and has promised even greater gifts.

* As servants we have nothing to glory of. (1Cor. 9:16)

* True servants of God never think they have done enough. (10)

* When we have done all we can as servants, we are still only vessels. (10)

* Unprofitable servants may not be useless but they are needless. (10)

* Christ is the Rock of Offense and a Stumbling Stone to many.

Reconciling Faith

LUKE 15:11-24

Introduction:

Our lesson today is part of a trilogy of the lost:

The lost sheep   Luke 15:3-7

The lost coin   Luke 15:8-10

The lost son   Luke 15:11-24

Each of these odes to the lost culminates with joy.

The term reconciled in the subject means to establish peace again.

Jesus is here speaking to tax collecters and others, who were considered to be sinners, traitors, and outcasts that were gathered to hear Him.

Jesus is speaking in a parable about a prodigal who was extravagant, lavish and wasteful; we could call him a spendthrift.

In each case of the trilogies, the owners that had lost something were self sacrificing and caring. In this case there was an impatient, optimistic, ambitious youth.

· ·

Translation, Transliteration, Interpretation:

11) All men are created on an equal level before God.

Men may be reared under the same roof but turn out different: as Cain and Abel, Jacob/ Esau Absalom and Solomon.

12) God is father to all men by Creation, but not by re-creation.

The portion ... That falleth to me; this was a presumption based on tradition which looked to a father's death, at which time the younger of two sons would receive 1/3 of inheritance. This father had not yet passed away but this son was anticipating/ taking for granted.

12) Falleth to me, επιβαλλον epiballon, I will inherit (Deut. 21:17)

Divided, διαιρεο diaireo, to cut assunder

* It seems like this son was unthankful, and forgetful that his father had some rights too.
* It is a mistake to think that gifts are debts.
* Here was a sad severance of an internal family bond

13) Αποδεμεο apodemeo, away from home

12) His living, βιον bion, goods, substance, means

13) Wasted, διασκορπιζω diaskorpizo, to winnow grain, scatter, opposite of gather

Riotous, ασωτως asotos, not to save, dissolute, sinful excesses, spend thrift

14, spent, δαπανησαντος depanesantos, to expend, consume, squander (Luke 14:28-30)

Famine, λιμος limos (when the boy was in need, the land was also in need)

* A famine is like a shepherd seeking lost sheep
* Sinners should thank God for rough warnings
* Calamities in this sinful world are visitations of God's mercy
* The young man's misery was general, but God's aim was personal
* There was a famine of truth in the boy's heart before it got to the land

14) To be in want, υστερος ustereo, to fall short, to fail to attain, to lack

15) Joined himself, εκολλαω ekollao, to glue together, cleave, passively he was glued

Citizen, πολιτον politon, from polis meaning city

* feeding swine was a degrading occupation for a Jew. This animal was considered unclean

* A prodigal will soon become a beggar

* This famine had not yet reached the citizen.

16) Fain, επεθυμει epethumei, to long for

Husks, κερας keras, called horns because of the shape of the pods which hung from the carab or locust tree; having a sweet taste. It is said that John the Baptist fed from these pods. From Locust Trees. They are still eaten today.

17) He came to himself, he had been beside himself, or out of his head

Hired servants, μισθος misthos, to hire, (obviously a wealthy home with servants.

Loaves to spare, περισσος perissos, around, surrounded by loaves

I perish, απολλομαι apollumai, contrast of loaves to spare

With hunger, λιμος limos, with famine, scarcity of food

18) I have sinned, ημαρτον emarton, to miss the mark

Before thee, ενοπιον enopion, in the sphere of thought

19) Worthy, αξιος axios, deserving

• •

Practical lessons:
*   Many youth, want to get as far away as they can from home and parents. (13)
*   He burned all his bridges behind him. (13)
*   Prodigals soon become beggars (14)
*   Wicked lust makes slaves of all men. (13)
*   Satan is a citizen of the world and many will join him in worldliness. (15)
*   Money makes good servants but bad masters.
*   Before returning to God one must return to self. (17)
*   Conviction is not conversion but it is in the right direction. (17)
*   There is room in our Father's heart as well as in His house. (22)
*   Parents have been young and what young people go through today is not surprising. (20)
*   Our Father God is willing to forgive the penitent and restore them. (20)
*   Independence from God is the root of all evil. (12)
*   A license to sin is a most perilous liberty. (13)

Healing Faith

LK. 7:1-10

Introduction:

Luke is the writer of today's lesson; the treatise is addressed to his acquaintance Theophilus. In the writing, Jesus has just concluded His sermon on the mount and has now departed to Capernaum, He used this large city for His headquarters in His Galilean ministry.

This city had many rich inhabitants and was located on the North West shore of the sea.

Consequently, there was a contingent of Roman Soldiers stationed there.

Matthew 8:5-13 is a parallel passage; he amplifies the event by saying that the servant was sick of the palsy, and that his master was the one who came to Jesus himself.

· ·

Translation, Transliteration, Interpretation:

2) Centurions played a great part in the gospel writing: one was in charge of the crucifixion another confirmed Jesus' death Mk. 15:44 one confirmed Jesus' Divinity Mk. 15:39 Cornelius was the 1st Gentile saved Acts 10

2) Ready, ημελλεν emellen, was about to

To die, τελευταν teleutan, to die

3) Heard of Jesus, δε περι του de peri tou

* Probably hearing of His healing Lk. 4:31-34, Lk. 5:17, 8:14; maybe hesitant to ask

Elders, πρεσβυτέρους presbutérous, leading citizens, maybe officers of the Synagogue

* Not normally supportive of Jesus, but they knew He could heal

218

* Here was a picture of attitudes: the Jews attitude to Jesus and to the Romans

The Roman attitude to Jesus
Jesus' attitude to the Jews and to the Roman; also the sick
The Jews' and Jesus' attitude to the forbidding law

Beseeching, ερωτων eroton, begging, asking, requesting

* Maybe they were thinking that Jesus was prejudiced as some of the Jews were

4) Instantly, σπουδη spoude, diligently, with haste

Worthy, αξιός axiós, deserving, of value, suitable, becoming

5) Loveth, αγαπα agapa, generous, faithful toward

Built, οικοδομεω oikodomeo, to construct

* The Romans had a history of desecrating and destroying Synagogues rather than building them
* Jesus would go, not because of the Synagogue but because of the faith of the Centurion

6) Trouble not, μη σκύλλω me skúllo, vex not, annoy not

* He was having 2nd thoughts of moral and spiritual unworthiness (unfit in or out of the house.)

7) He recognized Jesus' authority (He had all authority given unto Him in heaven and earth)

* His house could have been a noble mansion and still be unworthy for Jesus' entrance

Say in a word, ειπε λογω eipe (say) logo (by a word) this was different from Naaman in the O.T.

8) Set, τασσω Tasso, arranged, appointed

9) marvelled, θαυμα thauma, wonder, admiration

So great, τοσουτος tosoutos, more, so much, so many

10) Whole, υγιαινω ugiaino, in good health, hale, sound

* This Gentile's faith surpassed their faith

Practical lessons:
* This sick slave had the best physician; so do we (with Jesus)
* Both life and death are in His hands. 2, 7, 10
* We, His people, know how to get in touch with the Lord. (3)
* We are blessed to have elders who will intercede for us. (3, 4, 5)
* Kindness and respect can overcome human barriers. (4, 5)
* People in high positions can still be humble, especially to the Lord; and generous to the poor. (5)
* We should always approach Jesus with humility and awe, for He is awesome (6, 7)
* This man received Jesus in his heart even if not in His home. (7)
* Our Lord expects this kind of faith from His people. (Like the woman of Cana)
* It is never too late or too little to bring to the Lord in prayer. (6)
* We are not worthy but our Lord is worthy to be praised. (7)
* When we do acts of kindness others may not acknowledge them but our Lord is aware of them. (4, 5)
* Genuine faith delights out Lord. (9)
* Christ is not limited to Capernaum but is Christocentric.
* Today the same power is available to followers of the Lord.
* We should glorify Him by thinking, trusting, thanking, and telling
* By putting our life in His hands, we are being made whole. (10)
* God does not despise weak faith but loves strong faith more. (10)
* There is no misery too great for mercy. (10)
* This slave was healed on the master's faith. (10)
* Great faith in the Lord is healing faith. (9, 10)

Powerful Faith

MARK 9:14-29

Introduction:

Throughout this series we will be studying about faith from the gospel recorded by Mark.

Mark's Hebrew name was John or Johanan. He, being an understudy of Peter, who was an eye witness of Jesus, wrote about his servanthood. (See 1 Peter 5:13)

Col. 4:10 Mark is said to be nephew to Barnabas. Mark, traveling with Paul and Barnabas, turned back from them at Perga Acts 13:13.

The name Markus is said to be Greek, and his writing is one of the earliest of the New Testament written from Rome perhaps A.D. 68.

In the text Jesus had taken Peter, James, and John with Himself up on a mountain; there He was transfigured before them. Upon returning therefrom they found the other nine disciples being questioned by the scribes.

• •

Translation, Transliteration, Interpretation:

15) Straightway, υθεος utheos, without delay. This seems to be one of his favorite words

Amazed, εζεθαμβηθη ezethambethe greatly surprised.

Saluted, ησπαζοντο espazonto, greeted

16) Question, συζητεω suzeteo, investigative discussion

17) Master, διδασκαλε didaskale, teacher

Dumb spirit, αλαλον alalon, unable to speak. Matthew 17:15 says he was a lunatic.

18) Teareth, ρεσσει ressei, dashes down, tears assunder

Foam, αφριζει aphrizei, grindeth

Gnasheth, τριζει trizei, making a shrill cry or squeak

Pineth, ζηραινετα zenainetai, withering away, drying as grass (Jas. 1:4)

Cast him out, εκβαλωσιν, ekbalosin, (exorcism)

* The young man was having an epilepsy spasm or fit, plus being demon possessed.

19) Faithless, απιστος apistos, unbelieving (Matt. 17:20 little faith)

Suffer you, ανεξομαι anexomai, bear with you

20) Wallowed, κυλινοω kulinoo, was rolled

Tear Him, εσπαραζεν esparazen, threw into convulsion

Foaming, αφριζον aphrizon (see vs. 18)

* To destroy (Satan's purpose is to steal, kill, and destroy) apoleon

22, compassion on <u>us</u>, σπλαγχγισθεις splagchnistheis, move with pity

Help βοηθεσον boetheson, run, and succour

25) Running together, επισυντρεχει episuntrechei, rapid gathering

Foul, unclean akathartps
Dumb, αλαλον alalon, unable to talk. Deaf κοφον kophon, unable to hear

• •

Practical lessons:
* There are some who take a keen interest in the failure of Christians. (14)
* Jesus appeared when no one was expecting Him. (15)
* The nine disciples were embarrassed. (16)
* We fail God but He won't fail us. (18)

* The disciples were like the generation in which they lived; rather then changing it.

* We can always count on Jesus when others fail us. (18)

* Satan is a specialist when it comes to victimizing the weak. (22)

* This father made the son's case his own when he said <u>help us</u>. (22)

The syrophenician woman made her daughter's case her own. (Matt. 22, 25)

The leper said "if thou wilt" (Mk. 1:40) this man said "if thou canst" (22)

* The disciples failed because they were prayerless. (18, 29) prayerlessness makes powerless

* Complacency spells defeat. (18, 29)

* There was too much faith in self and not enough in Christ. (18, 19)

* Demons get into children too. (21)

* Demons can do a lot of damage and cause us to damage ourselves and others. (22)

* Where human strength fails, prayer prevails. (28, 29)

* On the mountain top is not where our work is; but in the valley. (9:5)

* While waiting for Jesus we will meet challenges. (9:14)

Where did the demon go when he came out of the boy?

* The disciples had cast out demons before, why not now?

The Consequences of Disobediences

ZEPHANIAH 3:1-8

Introduction:

Our lesson today will show that Israel had promised God <u>unconditionally</u> to obey His laws ex. 19:1 God had promised Israel to bless them <u>conditionally</u> Lev. 6-27

God had called Israel by the prophets but His call was refused. (2 Chron. 13:15, 16; 1ki. 22:10-14; Eze. 13:17; Matt. 24:11, 20:29-31; 1Jn. 4:1.

The consequences of God's Judgement (The Day of The Lord) was just 50 years (a generation) away.

The outline of today's lesson: Sins against the Lord 3:1-14

The Testimony of the Lord 3:5, 6

Rejection of the Lord 3:7, 8

• •

Translation, Transliteration, Interpretation:

1) Filthy, Mara, rebellion

Polluted, Gaal, unclean, defiled, profane

2) received (not), Laqach, to take

3) Roaring lions, this is a metaphor. The term roaring may infer hungry or boasting

Evening wolves is also a figure of speech inferring jackals that are dangerous, coming out at night. This reference was in reference to the priests that had polluted the sanctuary gnaw, Garam, to eat away, bite with intent to consume

Morrow, Boqer, the idea here is that the wolves would leave nothing for the next day. The priests, like beasts were egotistic and selfish.

4) Light, this term has several meanings. Here it means reckless, (like chaff) easily blown away in vs. 5 bring to light means to show or cause to appear.

Treacherous, bogedoth, deceptive, untrustworthy

(Done) violence, Gozal, distortion, take by suffering, snatch away

5) (Do) iniquity, Avlah, perversity

(Bring) judgement, Mishpat, to sentence (here is another metaphor)

Shame, Bosheth, embarrassment, contempt, disgrace

6) cut off, Karath, cut down

Passeth by, Abar, pass over

7) Corrupted, Shachath, suggests bringing into a worse state, defiling

8) Wait ye, Chakeh, the term <u>therefore</u> indicates the negative, stand still, watch, lookout, expect

Prey, Ad, spoil or booty

Assemble, Moed, to appoint a meeting

8) Pour, Shaphak, to shed out

Indignation, zoam, insolence

Fierce anger, Aph, snorting

Devoured, Akal, to consume, to eat up

Fire of my jealousy, Esh, (metaphoric) kindle, burning, blazing

• •

* Disobedience to God has dangerous consequences.
* God's day of reckoning is certain. (7)
* The Day of the Lord (judgement) was not limited to Israel but to all of their enemies: Philistines on the West, Moab and Ammon on the East, Ethiopia on the South, Assyria North. See 2 Chr. 12:3, 14:12, 13, 16:8; Jer. 13:23, 46:9, 13:23; Isaiah 20:4
* Jerusalem was called The City of Peace but God called it the oppressive city. See Ps. 83 Zeph. 3:1
* Idolatry carries the filth of pollution along with it. (1)
* Just because the consequences of sin may not be immediate, those doesn't mean they are not coming and that we should ignore God's warnings.
* God chastised Israel to teach them a lesson but they failed the test.
* With Israel "seeing was believing" but even seeing is not always believing; unbelievers don't believe even when they see.
* The fact that God was in their midst made their sins more detestable and judgement more deserving. (5)
* We must not give up on those who seem to be beyond God's grace. Isaiah 19:19, 23-25
* Many people, like sinful Israel, rise up early to do wrong, and stay up late at night to continue.
* After ignoring God there is nothing left but to wait for His judgment (8)
* When the guilty and un-repenting wait for God's judgement, it's not a pleasant wait. (8)
* The final day of the Lord is on it's way. Rev. 19:11
* It is self deception to think that God is pleased with the outside of the cup when the inside is full of pollution. (3;1, 2)
* Even when the world ignores God, He's still at work in it. (5)
* Leaders are responsible to God for the example they set before others. (3)

The Cleansing of the Temple

ISAIAH 56:6, 7; JER. 7:9-11; MK. 11:15-19

Introduction:
In the lesson today, we see how soon worthy initiatives can be corrupted.

In the Prophecy of Isaiah, we note:

The Ministry of the Messiah Ch. 47-57

The Suffering Survant Ch. 54-57

His Spiritual Blessings Ch. 56

Isaiah's vision carries forward to the Millennium

56:1) the Lord's salvation near to come

Available to those previously left out

Eunuchs were forbidden to worship in the assembly, Deut. 23:1-8

Now they have access

56:6) sons of strangers (foreigners) accepted fully as servants

56:2, 4) strangers will keep the Sabbath and the covenant

Ex. 31:12-17) the Sabbath was a key sign of the Jew's covenant

20:12-20

Isaiah 56:7) the Lord promises the non-Israelite worshipers of Vs. 6

Isaiah 56:8) the gathering is now being fulfilled. Rom. 10:12, 13; Eph. 2:13-18

56:7) The Holy Mountain is the Millenial Temple. Isaiah 2:2, 11:9, 65:25; Jer. 3:17

All people are joyful in the house of prayer.

Although Solomon prayed, this was not true of Solomon's Temple 1Kings 8:42

Gal. 3:28) Christ's death removed the barriers (Col. 3:11)

Isaiah 56:7) burnt offerings on the altar

Animal sacrifice in the Millennium

God's house, a house of prayer

Jeremiah 7:9, 11) Judah's false religion

1 Chron. 36:5-8) the ungodly reign of Jehoikim

7:4) Jeremiah denounced their contention that the presence of the Temple would keep Judah from harm.

Only godly deeds, not ceremonial observance would please God and preserve them.

Their profession and their conduct did'nt match. (Violation of Decalogue.)

Jer. 7:9)

They burned incense to Baal

*   They handled the Temple as a good luck charm

Jer. 7:11) the Temple was defiled

The Temple was called by God's name but the people calling it such were not His. 7:10, 14, 30, 32, 34

1 Kings. 8:12-21) Solomon's intent when He built the Temple was that it be a house of prayer.

The Temple was defiled by Ahab's daughter and sons

2 Chr. 28:24; 1 Kings 16:10-14) Temple doors closed (King Ahaz)

2 Chr. 29:17) doors reopened by Hezekiah

2 Chr. 33:4, 5) desecrated by Manesseh

2 Chr. 34:3, 4) cleaned by Josiah

Jer. 7:30) polluted again
7:11) den of robbers

* Hypocrites used the Temple as an asylum

God sees and knows the motives behind the actions

At Shiloh the sinful Jews were expecting victory, priests were killed & Ark was taken, 1 Sam 4

Mk. 11:15-19

Jesus in Temple looks around (it was late) He returned to Bethany
He came back the next morning and found corruption (15)
Cleansed Temple again, the 2nd time (Jn. 2:13-22)
In Gentile outer court (priests had Ok'd easy to buy animals rather than bring them).
Greek and Roman coins were exchanged by less than their value
Mk. 11:16) there was walking through the Temple as a short cut

* The Lord's house was to be a house of prayer for all people (Ethiopian Eunuch)
* Sounds of haggling and the smell of animals was very prominent
* The Temple had become a den of thieves (Jer. 7:11; Mk. 11:17)
* Robbers used the Temple as a hide out
* Gentiles were robbed of the opportunity to worship

* Jesus asserted His authority
* Jews would soon challenge His authority (Mk. 11:27, 28)

In the evening Jesus and disciples left the city and returned to Bethany (Mk. 11:11; Luke 21:37)

* Jesus showed His zeal for His Father's house

• •

Practical lessons:

* Only the arrogant expect God to overlook their unconfessed sins. (Jer. 9:7-9)
* We should never hesitate to assert our faith firmly, (Mk. 11:15, 16)
* Those who oppose Christ's truths do not accept Him as their Lord. (Mk. 11:18)
* Our attitudes are just as important as our deeds.
* After cleansing the Temple, the blind and deaf came to Him, and He healed them. (Matt 21:14)

The Feast of Weeks
LEV. 23:15-22

Introduction:

God had given to the Jews several feast days, all of which were typical of Christ in some way.

There was the Passover which was a type of redemption

The Feast of Unleavened Bread which was a type of communion with Christ

The Feast of Tabernacles or booths symbolizing the wilderness hardship in journeying

The Day of Atonement which symbolized repentance necessary before salvation

The Feast of Trumpets was a symbol of ingathering

The Feast of First Fruits was typical of Christ, and they that are His at His coming resurrection

The Feast of Weeks enlists our study today

This is called Feast of Weeks Shavuot because it was held 7 weeks after Passover or 50 days

It is also called Pentecost, First Fruits
See Num. 28:26; Exod. .23:16; Deut. 16:10; Acts 2:1, 20:16; 1 Cor. 16:8
This symbolized the coming of the Holy Spirit upon the early Church

* Our lesson also depicts several kinds of offerings to God, symbolizing indebtedness to Him.

The wave offering would symbolize the First Fruit of the Barley Harvest

The meat offering was not referring to meat but to grain

The burnt offering included an animal which was to be burnt on the altar for sin.

The drink offering was made of wine which was to be poured on the sacrifice. See Num. 15:10

The sin offering was offered for sin committed whether knowingly or unknowingly 23:19; Num 28:30

The peace offering was an expression of thanksgiving and a declaration of fellowship with God.

It accompanied a fulfillment of a vow or a free will for a specific blessing 19:5; Lev. 7:28

The offerer would eat the remaining portion with the family. Deut. 12:10-12 & priests see Deut. 7:29-34.

*   The Jews were forbidened to eat of any new harvest until it had been offered to God 23:14

*   No one was to appear before the Lord empty. Deut. 16:10

*   The grain offerings were not enough but were to be offered connected to blood sacrifice

*   The new Meat Offering of the Grain Sheaf was of Barley but the 2 loaves were baked of wheat

*   the 2 wave loaves were baked with <u>leaven</u> which, being a symbol of evil could never be offered and was not a symbol of Christ but only a symbol of the sinfulness of the people.

17) The word deal inferred an Ephah which was about 1/2 bushel

*   The sheaf was waved at the beginning of the harvest but the baked loaves offered at the end of harvest.

* The wave offering would be waved toward the altar back and forth many times.

Practical lessons:
* Worshipers of God who bring offerings are offering themselves as well.

Rom. 12:1, 2 ......present your bodies a living sacrifice, wholly and acceptable to God.
* No one can win God's favour with only good works.
* Offerings accepted by God are a Sweet Savour. (18)
* If we say we have fellowship with Him and walk in darkness we lie and do not the truth. 1 John. 1:6; Heb. 9:22-28
* The land belongs to God therefore any thing that comes from it also belongs to Him. (17)
* Christ is the first fruit from the grave. When He ascended He took some additional first fruit to wave before God. The believers are the rest of the harvest. Matt. 27:51-53
* 50 days from the Pass over 3000 new souls were brought into the kingdom of God. Acts 2:41
* Christians can help end starvation by providing for the poor. (22)
* Gleanings were to be left in the field for the poor but they had to gather for themselves. (22)
* God deserves more than one Special Feast day.
* The grain harvest was expanded to include olives and vineyards. Deut. 24:19-21
* The poor, strangers, orphans, and widows are on God's special Benelovent list. (22) 19:9, 10
* God is pleased when we recognize where our blessings come from and when we wave them back to Him. (18)
* God identifies Himself so there can be no mistake. (22)

The Day of Atonement

LEV. 16:11-19

Introduction:

The Day of Atonement (Yom Kippur), was observed on the 10th day of the 7th month (Tisri) and was to be observed for 24 hours. It occurred 10 days after "Rosh Hashanah" which was the New Year. The Day of Atonement occurs in October and portrays God's grace toward His people, cleansing them, and removing sin from His sight. On this day the Hebrews were to afflict their souls (Lev. 23:27) sorrowing for sin, with fasting.

To atone means to make reparation or amends for an injury done or implied.

It means to make expiation or satisfaction for recompense

The Hebrew word, Licaphar means "to cover" the idea being to cover sin.

Sin is a revolt against God's holiness, destroying fellowship with Him.

Trying to restore fellowship with God by good deeds and religious observance is useless/vain. God's grace provides a way for sinners who trust Him to be reconciled to Him. (Thru Christ). Before Christ the annual day of atonement prefigured Him who propitiated God for us. Because Heb. 10:4 relates that it was not possible that the blood of bulls and goats should take away sin. And Heb. 10:1 says that the law with its sacrifices which were offered continually was insufficient in achieving perfection. (See Rom.3:25)

The lesson text today can be understood or outlined as follows:

Vs. 11-14 atonement for the priest

Vs. 15-17 atonement for the people

Vs. 18-19 atonement for the altar

• •

Interpretation:

11) A bullock was an ox or a castrated steer.

*   This offering was for <u>himself</u>.

12) A censer was a pan made of copper, brass, or sometimes gold. Ex. 27:3; 2 Chr. 4:22

Sweet incense was made from stacte, onycha, galbanum, frankincense. Ex. 30:34-38

There was to be no substitute and this mixture was not to be duplicated for personal use. Ex. 30:38

Coals were not mineral coal but maybe charcoal or wool embers.

13) That he died not; the priest would take the incense into the most Holy place behind the vail with the fire and sprinkle it on the ground beneath the altar of testimony and burn the incense. It would make a thick cloud covering the mercy seat. The priest would not die by looking on the mercy seat because it was hidden from his eyes.

The testimony referred to the 2 tables of stone that were in the ark under the Mercy Seat.

*   The priest had to be very discrete in carrying these instructions out.

*   This was one of the reasons that 2 of Aarons' sons (Nadab & Abihu) were killed also John the Baptist's father Zacharias had a problem with his attitude behind the curtain/vail

14) The bullock's blood was to be sprinkled with the finger upon the mercy seat eastward or toward the front of the Mercy Seat seven times (intimating completion)

Heb. 9:6, 7 the high priest went into the Holy place only once per year. At other times he went up to the curtain to sprinkle blood Lev. 4:6, 17

15) Lev. 16:7, 8 two goats were selected and lots were cast to decide which one would be the scape goat, and which would be to offer to the Lord for the sin offering (9)

The same procedure was done for the atonement of the people as was done for the priest.

*   The sin offering which atoned for the sins of the priest was not necessary for the priesthood of Christ. (Heb. 7:26-28)

This goat was for the atonement of the people (16, 17)

18, 19) the blood of the bull and the goat was also offered for the atonement of the altar which was polluted by the sinful people.

This blood was put on the horns of the Altar, scapegoat, sacrifice goat to carry our sin, and cover our sin

• •

Practical lessons:
* Sinners are responsible to seek forgiveness from God for their sin. (11, 12)
* Sin always leads to death. (13) Rom? 6:23
* Sin is so terrible that it requires the shedding of blood for its remission. (14, 15) Heb. 9:22
* Sin taints everything that it touches. (16)
* Only God's designated one could enter into His presence and make atonement. (17)
* Aaron was warned only to enter the Holy Place at God's appointed time, in the proper manner, and attire. (16:29, 30) and with the designated sacrifices.
* There was no atonement designated for defiant sin, only unintentional and inadvertant. (15)
* The Church needs a house cleaning. It and the people are polluted. (18, 19)
* Only the priest stood between the people and God. 1Tim. 2:5, 6; Heb. 9:11, 12; Matt. 26:36-46, Matt. 27:46
* It is ironic that the altar which was used all the year would have to be atoned for. (18, 19)
* The continuity of sacrifices proved that sin had not been taken away. Heb. 10:1-4
* Christ ended the cycle of sin offerings. Heb. 9:24-28
* Christ is our scape goat who took away our sin.
* On the Day of Atonement many Hebrews wear white symbolizing purity and reading Isaiah 1:18
* Jesus has atoned for our sin and we should never forget our indebtedness to Him and to God for sending Him.

The Lord's Day

EX. 20:8-11, 31:12-16

Introduction:

The lesson today is from the forth commandment which is the longest of the Decalogue which would verify man's relationship to God who commanded it's keeping.

This is the one that men seem to argue over the most and try to separate from the rest.

This commandment was just as binding as the one condemning adultery or murder.

Numbers 15:32-36 tells of a man who gathered sticks on the Sabbath day after being commanded to abstain from necessary work. This man was commanded by God to be stoned.

When God provided manna in the wilderness for the Jews, they were not to gather the bread on the Sabbath day but were to gather enough to compensate on the day before. Ex. 16:22-30

Jesus would say later that the Sabbath was made for man and not man for the Sabbath. Mk. 2:27, 28 there was one 24-hour day per week called the Sabbath day and Jesus observed each in the Temple or the Synagogue.

• •

Translation, transliteration, interpretation:

8) Remember, Zakar, imprint

* God was reminding them of something that they already knew.

* This remembering was on God's authority

* This day was set apart for Holy Convocation. Lev. 23:7-13, study, meditation, worship, prayer.

Sabbath, Shabath, cessation

Day, Yom

9) Six, Shisha

10) Seventh, Shibiyi

11) Rested, Nuach, be at rest

Hallow, Quadesh set apart

31:13) keep, Shamar, watch, practice, observe, guard, heed, hold, and do

Sign, Oth, appointed

14) Defile, Goel, pollution, profane

* There were consequences for violating the Sabbath: Jer. 17:21-27; Neh. 13:15-22: Eze. 20:12-24

* "my sabbath, not yours" (13)

Cut off, Karath, cut down, assunder, destroyed

16) Perpetual, Olam, indefinite time, continuous, everlasting

• •

Practical lessons:
* God blessed and sanctified the Sabbath day; no such honor was given to the preceding days.
* This one day would give strength to the other six days. (11)
* Even the Land of Israel kept the Sabbath for 70 years while the Jews were in Babylon, 2 Chr. 36:21
* Many people think the Sabbath is no longer binding under the New Covenant but this is not so
* The Sabbath was not limited to the Jew only but to mankind.
* God gives blessings for keeping the Sabbath. Isaiah 58:13, 14
* The Sabbath day keeps man in contact with God (in true observance).

* The Sabbath day is like a paid vacation every seventh day.

* The Sabbath day was a type of the Sabbath Man. Col. 2:16, 17

* On the Sabbath day we are to renew our self offering to God. (Lev. 23:13)

* God's new converts and the world are watching our Sabbath day behavior.

* Observing the Sabbath day shows our relationship to God.

* Failing to keep the Sabbath day Holy is like stealing from God.

* God knows no weariness but is eternally content within Him, and He has symbolic rest for those who labor. Matt. 11:28

* The sixth day Creation was "good" therefore the Sabbath day is a memorial and a celebration.

* The Jews were given rest after 400 years of bondage in Egypt. Deut. 5:15

* Christ finished His work and after the resurrection took a Sabbath day's journey. Heb 4:1-10

* The Sabbath day no longer served as a covenant sign to us but a type of Christ. Col. 2:16, 17; Rom. 10:4; Gal. 3:19-26, 4:9

* The converted Jews of the first century accepted the change of the worship calander to the first day of the week.

* The Pharasees turned the day of rest into a straight jacket.

* The Sabbath day is like a doctor who gives His patient bed rest for one day, not for himself but for the patient's good.

* When Jesus arose on the first of the week He changed the Christian calendar to the first day of the week.

* Some persons rest the whole week without ever laboring.

* The Sabbath day is the Lord's Day because the day belongs to the one who made and purposed it. (13)

A Blessing for Ishmael and Isaac

GEN. 21:12-14, 17-21, 26:2-5, 12, 13

Introduction:

In the lesson today the fact is confirmed, God is in the blessing business, both of the righteous and the unrighteous. God honors His promise. God permits, prevents, directs, and determines the actions of men.

• •

Historical sketch:

God gave names both to IshmaelYshmael, meaning hearing, or God hears. Gen. 16:11

And Isaac, Yisichaq, meaning laughter Gen. 17:19

There was conflict between the two boys but especially between their mothers. Gen. 16:4, 5

One boy represented the flesh and the other the spirit Gal. 5:17

* Isaac represented the new birth (which is not an improvement of the old but the receiving of the New Nature).

* The carnal mind is enmity against God; it is not subject to the Law of God, neither indeed can be. Rom. 8:7. If this is so, then how can it be improved?

* The new birth is a passing from death unto life. John. 5:24.

* Abraham and Sarah had to be quickened before Isaac could be born. (New life)

* Both were beyond the reach of nature.

240

* Before anyone can be born again God must work a miracle, filling again the capacity that He made for Himself in man when He created Him.

* The new born must feed on the milk of God's Word in order to grow. 1 Pet. 2:2

* Ishmael was not cast out until Isaac was weaned. Gen. 21:8

* Ishmael and Hagar (both symbolic of persecuters) were cast out. (Gal. 4:28-31)

* As soon as Isaac showed up Ishmael showed out.

* When a believer in Christ obtains a new nature, he discovers the real character of the old nature.

• •

Translation, transliteration, interpretation:
21:12) Grevious, Yira, weighty, heavy

Lad, Naer, male child, young person

Called, Qara

* There was no need for Abraham to feel bad in putting his first son out; God was going to make him great also. And no harm would come to him in the wilderness.

21:14) Bread, Lechem, food, sustenance

Water, Mayim

Abraham had given her the child, now he is giving her sustenance.

14) Shoulder, Shekem, (on her shoulder perhaps as a sign of her servanthood)

Wandered, Taah, to go astray (some say that this meant she returned to her old ways of idolatry of her home land in Egypt.

15) Cast, Garash, abandoned. Shalak, to cause to go

* She cast the child under the shrubs.

17) Voice, Qol, sound

Aileth, Mah-lika, what to thee

19) Opened, Paqach (perhaps her eyes were holden (as was the 2 Emmaus Saints).

26:4) multiply, Rabah, make abundant

* Here are 6 more "I will's" of God's promises (28:2-4)

26:5) voice, charge, commandments, statutes, Laws, this verse is an example of Hebrew parallelism

Charge, Mishmereth, thing to be watched

* It is believed that 16:12 which says "he shall be against every man" indicates that Ishmael would become a robber and a fighter.

* Don't get confused with the "him" of 21:21, and the "him" of 26:2, one is Ishmael and the other is Isaac.

• •

Practical lessons:
* It is not unusual for God to pass His special blessings to the second born rather than to the first
* God's plan to bless one person does not preclude His blessings for another.
* Husbands should listen to their wives in the Lord when their demands are justified. (12)
* God wills that we say good bye to some people and places as Ur, Hagar; also sin)
* God hears our cries. (21:17)
* God can bring good out of evil.
* We ought not to curse whom God has blessed. (21:18)

Passover

EXODUS 12:1-14

Introduction:

Israel had been in slavery for four centuries in Egypt. God had already sent nine plagues to convince Pharaoh the King of His power and intentions to free His people the Jews. Pharaoh continued to rebel and God sent one last calamity. This tenth plague would convince him.

God called it His Passover. He had a unique status with the Jews and a special purpose for them. Again, it was the Lord's Passover. (Ex. 12:11)

• •

Translation, transliteration, interpretation:

2) Beginning of months: Abib Is said to be a Canaanite word meaning; newly ripened grain.

This first month would also be called Nisan. A Babylonian word meaning; to sprout or bud. This was the name of the Babylonian god of spring. (Neh. 2:6)

The Jews had two calendars: Abib, religious (our March/April
Tishri Cival (our Sept/Oct.)

The other months are as follows: Ziff/Iyar 1Kings. 6:1, 37) our month of May

Sivan (Esther 8:9)	our month of June
Tammuz	our July
Ab	our August
Elule (Neh. 6:15)	our September
Ethanim/Tisri (1Ki.8:2)	our October
Bul/Marcheshvan (1Ki.6:38)	our November
Chislev (Neh. 1:1); (Zech. 6:1)	our December
Tebeth (Esther 2:16)	our January
Sebat (Zech. 1:7)	our February

Adar (Esther 3:7, 8):   Our March

2nd Adar/Veadar

The Hebrew calendar includes 13 months and goes by the lunar year rather then the solar year

3) Congregation, Adar, an appointed assembly for a special purpose

* This is the earliest use of this word in the scripture

5) Blemish, Tamim, perfect, complete

From sheep or goats, some say that 2 Chron.35:7 relates that goats were used for this sacrifice others that only lambs blood was used.

6) Evening Ereb, some where between the 14th and the 15th day.

The lamb had been kept from the 10th to the 14th for <u>inspection</u>

7) Side posts, Mezuzah

Upper door post, Mashqoph, Lintel

8) In the <u>night</u>, Layelah

Roast with fire, Tsali, roasting

Unleavened bread, Matsah, without yeast Deut. 16:3 <u>Bread of Affliction</u>

Bitter herbs, Aseb miroriym

9) Raw, sodden, Na bashal, to boil or cook

(1) Adam sin is imputed to mankind

(2) Our sins are imputed to Christ

(3) Christ righteousness is imputed to us

Purtenances, Qereb, inward parts and heart

10) Burn, Saraph

* This is the same word for the Seraphim, fire dwellers, burning ones Isaiah 6:2)

11) Loins) Motinnayim, robes or loose clothing

Girded, Chagar, tucked in

Haste, Chippazon (12:34, 39)

12) gods of Egypt, there were many Egyptian idols. Jackals, Lions, Rams, bulls, goats, baboons

Execute, Asah, to carry out

13) Pass over, Pasach (neighbors couldn't carry blood with them or use others

Plague, Nageph, stumbling

14) Memorial, Zikkaron, remembrance

Ordinance, Chuqqah, a command, rule, law, etc.

● ●

* The Passover lamb was a type of Christ. 1 Cor. 5:7 Christ is the anti type

* The calendar is now dated not from His death but from His life.

* Christ was marked for death (days) before His death (3) 1Peter 1:19

* Nearly 4 years before His crucifixion He began His public ministry. (3, 6)

* No animal with blemish could propitiate God. (5) Lev. 22:21, 22

* one year represents the fact that Jesus was not too young nor too old but in fullness of manhood

* Jesus died at the exact time that pascal lambs were being slain in the Temple.

* Thousands of lambs were slain in Egypt but the word here is singular rather then plural.

* Ps. 102 confirm that Jesus was cut off in the midst of His days. (5)

* Vs. 3 says <u>a lamb</u> illustrating our unregenerated state

Vs. 4 says <u>the lamb</u> illustrating our recognition of Christ and our lost condition
Vs. 5 says <u>your lamb</u> illustrating our acceptance of the Lamb as our own personal Saviour

* It is interesting that the saved had to remain inside as it was with Noah's Ark, while the storm was passing over.

* <u>Adam's sin was imputed to man</u> (for all have sinned and come short of the glory of God)

<u>Our sins were imputed to Christ,</u> (we are bought with a price)
<u>Christ's righteousness is imputed to the believers,</u> (the Lord has laid on Him the sins us all) with His stripes we are healed

* Bitter herbs is a symbol of the remorse of our conscience, the guilt bringing about His suffering

* Redemption is complete with the blood of Jesus. Nothing else is needed. (10)

* Christ was made a curse for us. Gal. 3:13

The lamb was not to be eaten raw or in water because both of these conditions would hinder the roasting. (9)

* God's instructions are always exact in every detail. (5-10)

* We are to be ready to move when God says go. (11)

* God doesn't want us to forget His goodness as symbolized in the contents of the Ark of the Covenant. (14)

* Jesus had already typically been in Egypt in the first pass over, before eating the feast with His disciples. (Matt. 2:15)

* The side posts and the lentil were His pierced brow, nailed hands, and feet. (7)